GAMES THAT ● WORK

Co-operative Games and Activities
for the Primary School Classroom

SUSAN HILL

ELEANOR CURTAIN
PUBLISHING

First published in 1992
ELEANOR CURTAIN PUBLISHING
906 Malvern Road
Armadale 3146
Australia

Copyright © Susan Hill 1992

Reprinted 1992

National Library of Australia
Cataloguing-in-publication data:

Hill, Susan (Susan Elizabeth).
   Games that work: co-operative games and
   activities for the primary school classroom
   ISBN 1 875327 16 9

   1. Group work in education. 2. Group games —
   Study and teaching (Primary). 3. Games — Study
   and teaching (Primary). 4. Creative activities and
   seat work — Study and teaching (Primary). I. Title.
372.1395

Production by Sylvana Scannapiego,
   Island Graphics
Edited by Ruth Siems
Designed by Sarn Potter
Cover design by David Constable
Cover photograph by Sara Curtain
Photographs by Allan Moore and Robert Mastripolito
Typeset in 12/14 pt Baskerville
   by Optima Typesetting and Design, Melbourne
Printed in Australia by Impact Printing

Distributed in North America by:
Peguis Publishers
100-318 McDermot Avenue
Winnipeg, MB
Canada R3A 0A2

CONTENTS

For my daughter Alex Hill.

PREFACE

This collection of games and activities was prompted by watching my five-year-old daughter begin school. On that first day of school most children moved off easily and made friends. They had learned to join groups quickly. Others had much to learn. Several of the five year old boys and girls held tightly to their parent's legs, protesting with angry, red faces.

I draped myself against the walls of the classroom watching my daughter Alex as she observed the other children. My fingers and arms were crossed as I wished for her to make friends quickly and want to go to school.

Social skills are learned. They are not innate. Social skills affect how children approach their first days at school and, later, school and family life. Much of what happens in school centres on our social relationships, making friends, being accepted.

I hope these games and activities will help children work and play together more thoughtfully and with greater care for each other.

ACKNOWLEDGEMENTS

Grateful acknowledgment is made to the following: Jane O'Loughlin and the year seven class at Mercedes College for their suggestions about co-operative learning; Polly Eckert and the teachers and children at Taperoo Primary School for inspiration and commitment to co-operative learning; Marcia Lomman and Ann Speck, both students at the University of South Australia and Highgate Primary After School Care Co-ordinators, for their time and interest in the games and activities; Carole Cooper for a meeting where we discussed co-operative learning as a beginning place for changing the structure and behaviour within educational institutions so they become supportive educational communities.

Professor Robert Stake at the University of Illinois provided a quiet place to read, think and write. He shared some of the co-operative games he knew and clarified the idea that some competitive games can be fun but not when they are at the expense of others.

Several games were played at a Co-operative Learning Conference at Summerland Education Resource Centre, Goonebellah NSW October 1991. Thank you to the teachers involved and especially to Robyn Hunt who organised the conference and demonstrates commitment to education by giving freely in her work with people in schools.

I am grateful to the University of South Australia for providing professional experience leave and the time to write this book. Thanks to my colleagues at the University who have challenged, inspired and supported me for many years, in particular, Professor James Eaite who provided critical feedback and encouragement.

I would also like to gratefully acknowledge the support of Tim Hill who encouraged me to explore the academic and social benefits of co-operative learning.

This book is a co-operative effort. The publisher, editor, photographers, author, designers, children, teachers, colleagues and friends all played essential roles in creating this book. We do not do it alone.

Every effort has been made to acknowledge the source of these games and activities. Many games change each time they are played and many activities have been modified over time. The author apologises for any source omissions.

PART ONE

LEARNING FROM
EACH OTHER

LEARNING TOGETHER

We learn and relearn the importance of relationships in communicating and working together. We seek out people who will challenge our thinking and support us in our projects, and we are drawn to those who gently remind us to give as well as to take, for it is people who make the difference to our quality of life.

We are social beings. We learn by communicating with others through our senses of hearing, sight, touch, taste and smell. It is the contact and feedback from others that nurtures these senses, sharpens our vision and intensifies and refines our thoughts. The way we know ourselves is through others, and our view of ourselves is intimately tied to the relationships we have with others.

We know about the studies of feral children and those kept in isolation who are unable to speak, intellectually stunted by the lack of social interaction. We work towards providing caring, nurturing, collaborative communities in which children and adults can learn. As educators we have a vision of a co-operative learning community which is dynamic, not passive, where conflict, when it occurs, is viewed positively and resolved co-operatively.

Learning to work collaboratively is not limited to teaching a small set of skills in a social skills program. We don't learn to co-operate by reading cute animal posters, 'Happiness is being friendly'. Collaborating with others does call on co-operative skills, like ways to negotiate, but rather than being a small part of a program to be tacked on to an existing curriculum, co-operative learning permeates everything we do. It is a way of life and the heart of a school curriculum.

THE BENEFITS OF CO-OPERATIVE LEARNING

Learning involves constructing knowledge and is most challenging, engaging and active when groups of mixed ability, gender, age, ethnic and socio-economic backgrounds work together. The construction of knowledge, as opposed to the transmission of knowledge in one direction from teacher to student, involves testing ideas and building conceptual frameworks with others through dialogue and critical debate (Wells, Chang & Maher 1990). While teacher-to-child transmission of information, facts and ideas has a place in learning, it is only when we test, confirm, assimilate and accommodate ideas into our conceptual frameworks that knowledge takes on meaning (Piaget 1977).

The long-term academic and social benefits of co-operative learning are overwhelmingly positive (Slavin 1985, Johnson & Johnson 1989). Johnson and Johnson, in a summary of over one hundred and twenty research studies, point out that co-operative learning experiences tend to promote higher motivation to learn, especially intrinsic motivation, more positive attitudes towards teachers and learning, and higher academic achievement than competitive or individualistically organised classes.

The benefits of co-operative learning have been well documented. (Cohen 1990, Slavin 1989, Johnson & Johnson 1990)

- Co-operation leads to higher achievement.
- Co-operative learning facilitates deeper levels of understanding.
- Co-operative learning is more fun.
- Co-operative learning develops leadership skills.
- Co-operative learning promotes positive attitudes to school.
- Co-operative learning promotes self-esteem.
- Co-operative learning is inclusive learning.
- Co-operative learning brings about a sense of belonging.
- Co-operative skills are the skills of the future.

CO-OPERATIVE LEARNING GOALS

There are four major learning goals in planning any school curriculum: knowledge, skills, dispositions and feelings (Katz & Chard 1989). When we implement a curriculum based on the principles of co-operative learning, knowledge, skills, dispositions and feelings are important.

Knowledge involves information, facts, stories, myths and concepts and various schematic frameworks for further learning. We learn **skills** which are easily observable discrete units such as ways to join a group or listening to isolate a particular sound and its corresponding letter. As we learn we develop a **disposition** or tendency to respond in particular characteristic way like inquisitiveness and persistence. We also develop **feelings** of confidence, anxiety and feelings of being accepted (Katz & Chard 1989).

KNOWLEDGE

Important knowledge for children involves the notion of why it is important to work together rather than against each other.

Why are we working together? Why do we help all members of the group? Why is it important to include all members of the group in decisions and choices? The group is only strong if all work together. If we all learn from each other we have many, many teachers. It is best if all members win and go forward rather than having one person win and all the others lose.

What is valued as knowledge is largely a socio-cultural phenomenon. More and more we are valuing collaborative behaviours as we move away from the competitive industrial era where winning at all costs and tearing down or exploiting resources — whether people or materials

— was a matter of course. We are at the forefront of a new era, a post-industrial era. (Lankshear 1991)

When we learn collaboratively we gain **knowledge** of ways to work with others. We learn that co-operation works when there is a common purpose and goal. We learn that two heads are better than one. If a group has common goals and purposes, it can employ a range of useful strategies to get the job done. We learn that sometimes we play the role of organiser and at other times the encourager of others. We build up a useful repertoire of strategies. For example, a group creating a class newspaper or a garden may draw on knowledge of how groups can be structured to work together and various roles can be assigned, recorder, checker, material gatherer, organiser and more.

SKILLS

The **skills** for co-operating may be attentive listening or turn-taking, which underpin the more complex negotiation and mediation skills. A skill is a behaviour that has become automatic, like not all talking at once or using eye contact when listening to someone. Children often need to be cued to remember to take turns or use quiet voices.

Skill improves with practice and co-operative games and activities provide this practice. Young children can learn mediation skills to resolve disputes between two or more conflicting views in games like Coming to Consensus on page 73 by following a framework like:

- get the ideas out
- alternative solutions
- consequences
- consensus

DISPOSITIONS

Dispositions are habits or personality traits. Katz and Chard (1989) define dispositions as enduring habits of mind and action, or tendencies to respond to experiences with particular frequency.

A desirable disposition may include humour, gentleness, helpfulness and generosity. An undesirable disposition may include jealousy, avarice, violence and selfishness.

Building **dispositions**, or habits, about ways to behave while working and learning takes time. Sometimes children's dispositions when beginning school are co-operative and helpful. Sometimes children or a group of children have chosen to respond in a way that is attention seeking by being uncooperative.

The lives some children experience may not promote co-operative dispositions and learning to trust and work with others in school is done in steps over many years. For some children, distrusting others has proved to be the safest behaviour and the best way to take care of themselves.

FEELINGS

Children who have positive **feelings** about themselves are more likely to see others more positively (Laurence 1987). Self-esteem and confidence are linked to achievement, but a great artist may not be a skilful footballer. We all have strengths and weaknesses. To build self-esteem children can learn to recognise and affirm the strengths of others. Affirmations should not take the form of insincere lavish praise but should acknowledge weakness and provide specific feedback on strengths and constructive behaviour.

Interestingly, a body of research indicates that children with high self-esteem are not self-centred or self-important individuals; high self-esteem is associated with less egocentricity, more altruistic behaviour, sharing and generosity (Fountain 1990).

ASSESSMENT OF CO-OPERATIVE LEARNING

Co-operative learning requires assessment and feedback. Assessment of the use of co-operative behaviour can be managed in several ways: teacher assessment, group assessment or assessment by the individual student. The teacher, another adult or a student can observe co-operative behaviour for growth in knowledge, skills and children's positive feelings for each other. Regular feedback about co-operative skills reminds children to keep these skills high on their agenda even when absorbed in complex problem solving.

Many teachers remember to cue the group in advance to watch for both the content of *what* was learned in an academic area and *how* the group used co-operative behaviours.

Group and individual assessment can focus on how the group maintained and encouraged each other and the roles that specific individuals played. Goals for future learning grow out of this assessment.

THE PRINCIPLES OF CO-OPERATIVE LEARNING

Our curriculum planning for the four learning goals can be influenced by three basic goal structures: competitive, individualistic and co-operative, or hybrids of these (Katz & Chard 1989).

In a competitive goal structure, students work against each other and the probability of one student achieving a goal or reward is reduced by the presence of capable others.

In an individualistic goal structure, the probability of receiving a reward is unrelated to the capabilities of others. The task itself becomes the reward.

In a co-operative structure, the probability of one student receiving a reward is enhanced by the presence of capable others. These basic goal structures influence decisions about how we organise and work with groups and the projects, games and activities we provide for learning.

Co-operative groups	Traditional groups
positive interdependence	no positive interdependence
common group goals	individual goals
mixed ability groups	homogeneous groups
shared leadership	one appointed leader
frequently changing group membership	mostly static group membership
group and individual responsibility	responsible only for self
co-operative skills are explicit	co-operative skills assumed
group feedback and reflection	no group feedback on effectiveness

POSITIVE INTERDEPENDENCE

This occurs when games and activities are structured so that everyone has a role to play. Positive interdependence also occurs when the activity cannot take place unless everyone is engaged. A theatrical production is a good example of this. All group members have acting or production roles and all are essential. In partner work, dividing roles into listener and speaker makes for positive interdependence because both are needed.

STRUCTURING FOR POSITIVE INTERDEPENDENCE

There are ways we can organise learning groups so that each member of a pair or group has a role to play and the roles are interdependent. This way of organising is known as structuring for positive interdependence.

Think/pair/share

Students reflect for a minute or two on a question posed by the teacher. Then ideas are shared with a partner. The pair forms a group of four and ideas are shared round robin. The teacher then may ask individuals to share one idea given by themselves or their partner. (Kagan 1990)

EEKK

An acronym for eye to eye and knee to knee, it promotes face to face interaction. (Dishon & Wilson 1991)

Purple hats

This idea is based on de Bono's six thinking hats to generate different ways of thinking. An issue can be debated in groups of six with participants taking these different views. (de Bono 1991)

WHITE HAT: information facts only, not interpretations or arguments
RED HAT: emotions, feelings and intuitions
PURPLE HAT: negative, caution, judgement, criticism
YELLOW HAT: positive, optimistic view
GREEN HAT: creative, new ideas something that has not been said before
BLUE HAT: encouraging others, summarising what has been said

Three-step interview
Partners take turns to interview each other about a topic being studied.
1 Partner one interviews partner two.
2 Partner two interviews partner one.
3 Form a group of four and share ideas. (Kagan 1990)

Whip
A whip occurs when each participant is asked to reflect and give feedback on an issue discussed by the group. Sometimes a spokesperson, speaking for the group, contributes a new idea to a class list of ideas. (Graves & Graves 1990)

Pyramiding
After partner work, groups of four or six join together to pool ideas. The group may work towards consensus on an issue. (Graves & Graves 1990)

Huddle
Like a football huddle, groups join together to answer questions put by the teacher. They may also pose questions to ask other groups or the teacher. (Graves & Graves 1990)

Piggybacking
This is similar to the whip, but each person piggybacks on the response of the previous speaker by saying, 'I agree (or disagree) that . . .' then their own comments are added.

Co-operative reading
Partners take turns to read an agreed amount then ask each other questions to check for understanding.

Role reading
This idea is based on reciprocal reading (Palincsar & Brown 1985). The reading processes of predicting, questioning, clarifying and summarising are transformed into roles. Children work in groups of four in the various roles, then roles are switched. (Hill & Hill 1990)

Jigsaw
Questions or issues to be used as a basis for gathering information are brainstormed by the whole group. Expert groups or research groups

gather data and record it so that each person can go to a new group as an expert. The new group is a co-operative group made up of a range of experts from the original research groups.

When planning the groups it helps to work out the numbers carefully. If there are 20 children they can be placed in five expert groups and reform into four co-operative groups to share ideas. (Aronson 1971)

(Aronson et al. 1977)

COMMON GROUP GOALS

When academic content goals and co-operative goals are clarified and agreed upon, groups work more effectively. Often the best we can do is have broad, general goals that are close or similar. For example, in a class play at the end of the year the class may have one broad goal of putting on a great performance but individual members may have goals varying from pleasing the teacher to impressing parents or being a valued member of a team.

MIXED ABILITY GROUPS

Mixed ability groups encourage members to use co-operative skills when working together. Friendship groups can mean that friends can freeload on each other and protect each other from the teacher if the work has not been done. Homogeneous groups often mean that the less proficient students do not have academic and social role models. Gifted students use co-operative skills and high-level application level thinking when explaining ideas to those who may not grasp information as quickly.

SHARED LEADERSHIP

By breaking down the leadership roles into time keeper, recorder, summariser and so on, more people have an opportunity to practise leadership skills.

FREQUENTLY CHANGING GROUP MEMBERSHIP

As co-operative skills are called on more when working with others we do not know well, frequently changing group membership is essential. Sometimes a base group can meet regularly as a support group but, at other times, changing groups within the classroom promotes co-operation and class cohesion. The notion that we are all in this together is developed.

GROUP AND INDIVIDUAL RESPONSIBILITY

When a group works on a task, everyone in the group is responsible for contributing and not freeloading on other's efforts. Group members can support each other's contributions and provide time for regular feedback on how they worked as individuals and as a group.

CO-OPERATIVE SKILLS ARE MADE EXPLICIT

The following list of co-operative skills is a useful starting point for planning what skills to teach. Each of these co-operative skills can be made explicit before playing any of the games and activities in this book.

To make the skills explicit, for example active listening, the teacher may role play talking and listening with a class member. The rest of the class can sit in a circle, known as a fishbowl, and observe the listening behaviour.

Many teachers like to record the co-operative behaviours on Y-charts describing what the co-operative skills look like, sound like and feel like.

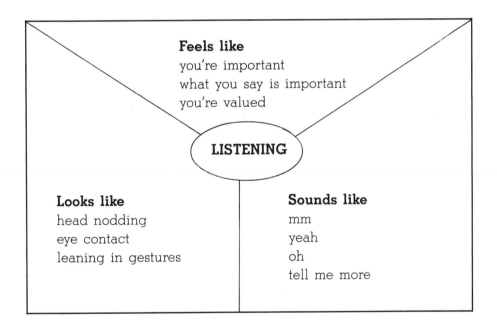

Feels like
you're important
what you say is important
you're valued

LISTENING

Looks like
head nodding
eye contact
leaning in gestures

Sounds like
mm
yeah
oh
tell me more

CO-OPERATIVE SKILLS

Forming groups
- making space for people
- making pairs or circles
- staying with the group
- keeping hands and feet to yourself
- forming groups without bothering others

Communication
- eye contact
- taking turns
- active listening
- using quiet voices
- using people's names
- eliminating put-downs

Working with group roles
- observer
- recorder
- summariser
- encourager
- clarifier
- organiser
- time keeper
- and more

Problem solving as a group
- defining the problem
- brainstorming
- clarifying ideas
- confirming ideas
- elaborating ideas
- seeing consequences
- criticising ideas
- organising information
- finding solutions

Managing differences
- stating position or problem
- seeing the problem from another view
- negotiating
- mediating
- reaching consensus

GROUP REFLECTION AND FEEDBACK

Finally, perhaps the most important aspect of co-operative learning is the way in which the group worked and learned together. As teachers we are familiar with providing feedback on the content of **what** was learnt but the process of **how** we learned, **how** we co-operated, requires continual feedback to reminded us to use co-operative skills. Goals for future learning can be set here, after feedback and reflection.

POSITIVE FEEDBACK
Providing positive feedback is essential in co-operative learning because the co-operative skills are isolated and made explicit. Feedback to each

person is as important as feedback to the group because knowing we belong to a group and are accepted encourages us to work effectively together.

It is particularly important for isolated or rejected children to know they are accepted as people and their strengths valued. Disruptive group members often seek attention as a way of confirming to themselves that they belong. Demonstrating that the group members value their place in the group helps allay fears of neglect or rejection.

Throughout the games and activities, feedback can be given when appropriate. Feedback at the end of each game will largely depend on what co-operative skills were used well during the activity.

USING CO-OPERATIVE GAMES AND ACTIVITIES

THE BENEFITS OF CO-OPERATIVE GAMES

Co-operative games and activities provide a way of learning and practising co-operative skills. The benefits of co-operative games are many.

ENERGISERS AND FUN

Co-operative games have many benefits but one of the best cases for including them in a curriculum program is that they are fun. We enjoy playing co-operatively. We laugh, tension is broken, and somehow energy is released.

INCLUDE OTHERS

When children make groups for games and projects, the socially competent children often select other socially competent children. The shy, withdrawn or aggressive children are not chosen. They are left to interact with the other children with less well developed social skills and this only reinforces their social difficulties. Many children try to enter groups by trying to take over only to be told to 'back off' or 'go play somewhere else'.

Joining groups to play games or work on projects involves negotiation and negotiation is communication both spoken and nonverbal. Fifty per cent of children's negotiations to join in are successful (Hill & Reed 1989). Those children who are often successful retain their self-esteem.

Children with low self-esteem and those children who have developed inappropriate co-operative strategies benefit from engaging in co-operative activities because time is provided for them to practise these social skills.

EVERYBODY WINS

Watch a circle of children playing a co-operative clapping game with one child in the middle demonstrating a clapping pattern. All participants want the game to continue. Everybody wins if the game continues because it is fun.

The activities in this book shift the focus from competition and scoring points at the expense of others to encouraging participating with others. We all have the right to be accepted and the right to belong in school groups, not because we are the best, the strongest, or the most hard working. Competition is not synonomous with having a good time. Children who want to win at all costs cannot maintain the advantage and suffer loss of esteem when they don't win.

Many people agree that competition is a fact of life. Many team sports emphasise competition, but closer examination of a football or netball team reveals that it is team-work that builds a strong united front. A successful football team plays as a team, encouraging its players to co-operate rather than play the game as individuals.

INCLUDING NOT ELIMINATING

Elimination games like musical chairs or circle murder, where the murderer winks at you and you pretend to die, teach children to compete. They may be fun for the quick and agile. The more awkward and less co-ordinated children are often 'out' on the first round. This creates a feeling of winning at the expense of others — not a positive feeling in the group. Barriers are created between people and thus everyone loses. When children and adults are not feeling particularly valued by the group, and they lose, they are less likely to be supportive members of the class.

TEACHER OR FACILITATOR PLAYS TOO

Participants get more involved if the game organiser joins in too. Children are amused watching their teacher play the lap game or trust falls. There is also a feeling of equality when everyone joins in.

HOW TO USE CO-OPERATIVE GAMES

Co-operative games can increase co-operative behaviour when they are used systematically over several weeks (Hill & Reed 1989). The games and activities can be used when conflict due to gender, race, class or ability differences occurs. In most of these games and activities, the individual class member becomes important as part of a team and the whole group succeeds when all members work together.

While co-operative games can be an addition to the school program, they are most effective as part of a total collaborative school program where more traditional hierarchical structures have become more democratic. These games and activities can be used in any curriculum area.

Co-operative games can be used as warm-ups to begin the day. Fifteen minutes set aside for co-operative games with careful instructions about how to work together sets up a caring, positive atmosphere. Some teachers use co-operative games after lunch and recess breaks to build a team or cohesive spirit.

Each co-operative game or activity can have the co-operative skills involved made clear and explicit before being practised. Feedback on how we worked is then discussed after the activity to retain the co-operative focus.

Co-operative skills are:
- **made explicit:**
Each game has a focus on particular co-operative skills. These skills can be made clear and explicit.
- **practised:**
The games and activities are the means by which the co-operative skills are practised.
- **given feedback:**
How we worked together and how I worked or played as an individual group member is discussed after each activity.

MODIFYING CO-OPERATIVE GAMES AND ACTIVITIES

Each time these games and activities are played, small changes are made to suit the age of the children and their experiences. Flexibility is necessary to adapt the games and activities. As teachers we make judgements to modify the games based on observation of how the children are performing.

Some of the co-operative games and activities are suited to very young players. Most activities can be modified to suit any age group.

Several games in this book were orginally designed as competitive games where one individual or team wins. For example, the original game of Musical Chairs is an elimination game with one winner at the end. Co-operative Musical Chairs demands team work so that all players are included as the chairs are removed.

PART TWO

CO-OPERATIVE GAMES
AND ACTIVITIES

FORMING GROUPS

HOW TO USE PART TWO

The games and activities in Part Two are organised under a framework of co-operative skills. This does not mean, however, that these skills are developed in isolation. When employing the co-operative skill of negotiating what we want to learn, we are also listening, turn-taking and making eye contact.

There will be many times when co-operation in groups breaks down, and this is the time to return to the simple co-operative skills, like listening. You could turn to the listening activities and games as a focus to reintroduce and practise this important skill.

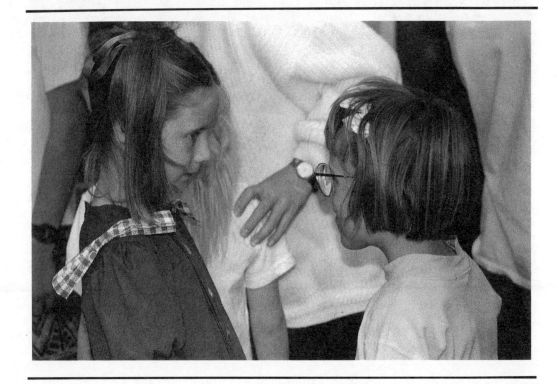

GETTING TO KNOW OTHERS

When new groups are formed, people are often reserved, tense and cautious. Quick warm-up games help break the ice and get people talking and finding out more about each other.

QUALITY INITIALS

This can be use to start off a group meeting. Everyone calls to mind their initials, either two or three: Tom Albert Hall could be TH or TAH. He then thinks of two (or three) affirming qualities to describe himself 'tremendous and hopeful'.

Finding affirming words to describe yourself starts the group out in a positive way.

LINE-UPS

This is a warm-up game making use of gentle touching and nonverbal communication. The aim is for the group to line up in order of birthdays with the first January birthday lined up by the door. Tell the participants that the day and month will be important. No one is to speak so the participants use nonverbal cues like finger signals, foot stamps and facial expressions to order themselves. When the group is in line they call out their birthday date, both day and month, to see how well they have nonverbally communicated the order of birthdays.

Young children enjoy line-ups from the tallest to the shortest and as teachers we are often surprised at the child or children who step out to become the class organiser placing people in order. It is best for the group to wait for this to happen rather than arranging leaders.

Other forms of nonverbal line-ups are:

- according to star sign
- according to age (this would suit a vacation program with mixed ages)
- by the number of buttons on your clothing
- by the number of letters in your name
- the length of your hair
- height of shoulders
- height of knees
- level of waist or belt, if one is worn
- the size of your shoes
- matching one colour from your clothing with the person on your right and another colour with the person on your left

Feedback: including others is the most important co-operative skill here. Space has to be made for all to fit in the line. Making a circle encourages participants to make space for others. (See Graves and Graves 1990 for more line-up ideas.)

GETTING ACQUAINTED

There is a series of activities here — but some activities help participants to share thoughts and feelings more than others. Talk about which discussion starters generate more risk-taking, trust and feedback from others.

The instructions for the activities are:

1 Everyone stand up and mill around the room making sure that you greet everyone in some nonverbal way a nod, a handshake, a smile, a touch on the arm or any other way you can think of to say hello.

2 Now sit down with a person you do not know well. Each person then takes one minute to introduce themselves and describe the kind of person they are.

3 Now find a new person you do not know well. Sit down with them and for one minute each discuss a peak experience you have had recently. This peak experience should be a positive experience. If you remember an experience that was negative, describe what was learnt from the experience.

4 Now find someone else you don't know and sit down with them. Share a fantasy or day-dream you often have. It could be connected with success like becoming prime minister, or it may be connected with finding a boyfriend or girlfriend and falling in love. Perhaps

your fantasy is going on a holiday or working in a team to create world peace.

5 Now form a new group of four people with as many people as possible that you have already talked to in the previous activities. Talk about:
- which activity was most helpful in getting to know the person you were interacting with
- which activity led to the most risk-taking, trust and openness.

Alternative topics to discuss are:
- What I remember about my childhood.
- What I want to improve about myself
- My impressions of you are . . . .
- If I could change the world I would . . . .
- If I were prime minister or president I would . . .

(Johnson & Johnson 1985)

GROUP INTERVIEWS

If the group has over twenty participants divide into two groups of ten. Each person then takes turns to be interviewed by the group members. The interviewee sits out the front with the group in a semicircle around them. The interviewee can choose the topic for the interview or simply answer questions about themselves from a range of areas interests, hopes, pets, family, history and more (Masheder 1990).

MAGIC CIRCLE

Divide into groups of five to seven people. Sit on the floor or on chairs in a circle. Take it in turns to randomly pull prepared cards from a hat. The cards have phrases such as:

'I feel good when . . . '
'The best thing that has happened to me is . . . '
'My greatest wish is . . . '
'Today I will . . . '

Sometimes the cards have simple words to start thoughts moving, words like *put-downs*, *friends* or *trust*, and each person in the group gives a sentence completion or explains what the word means to them.

Feedback: At the end of the session discuss which phrases or words were easiest to discuss and which words gave the most trouble.

QUICK WARM-UP

In a big group, a teacher or facilitator calls to participants to form pairs and hold hands. Next, threes are formed, again holding hands. Groups of fours, fives and sixes are made to practise forming groups of people who have not worked together previously. Then the group can be called to:

- form a new partnership and hold hands.
- form a line of people holding hands.
- move two steps apart.
- the top couple walks down between the pairs.
- as the couple moves through the two lines each pair touches them and says words of welcome.
- the game is complete when all members have passed down the line.

(Summerland Education Resource Centre 1991)

NAME GAMES
NAMES IN MOTION

The group stands in a circle. One person at a time comes into the middle of the circle and says their name accompanied by an action. The action can match the number of syllables in the name, both first and surnames. The action could be a jump, hand clap, swirls around and a high kick. The possibilities are endless.

For example, Samuel jumps into the centre and says Sam-u-el as he makes three movements, e.g. touch shoulders, clap hands then click fingers. The class, in unison, repeats the Sam's name and the action routines. Sam says *Again*, and repeats his name and the actions if the actions were not as accurate as he would have wanted. The person in the middle chooses another, and the process starts over again.

A variation is to have children in pairs decide on an action to suit their names, e.g., *Ben and Samantha*. The children then repeat the names and the actions. The action could be a simple swaying side to side. Alternatively, children may repeat the actions while keeping absolutely silent.

This is an affirming activity as the children have an opportunity to stand in the middle of the circle with everyone copying their actions.

NAME TAG MIX-UP

Write out name tags for each person and, when they enter the room, check their names off on a roster but give each person a different name tag. Participants can then find the person who has their name tag. They introduce themselves and switch over name tags. If the group is small enough the paired individuals can introduce each other to the group (Scannell & Newstrom 1983).

WHAT'S YOUR NAME?

Divide a group of twenty or so into groups of six to eight people. Have each group stand in a circle. Each group is given a soft ball or a bean bag, and as it is tossed from one person to another, the person holding the bag calls out their name. The ball is then tossed onto the next person. Continue this for five or so minutes until you think everyone in the group knows each person's name.

I saw this ball toss idea in a drama class where students stood in a circle and tossed balls between each other and repeated the lines, not always in order, they were learning for a play. This game acted as a rehearsal and the energy it took to throw and catch the ball provided extensive voice production exercises as lots of air was expressed in the throw (Scannell & Newstrom 1983).

TRUE AND FALSE

Hand out a name tag and invite the participants to write their names and three things that are true and one thing that is false about their personality or personal likes and dislikes. Name tags are pinned on and pairs are formed. The teacher or leader tells each pair they have three questions only to find out which idea is false.

After three questions each and finding the false statement, they switch partners and find someone they do not know at all or someone they have not spoken to. Partners can be switched until most have met everyone in the group.

It is best if participants ask general questions. For example if a participant has listed *I love eating all yellow vegetables*, the partner would ask, *What do you like to eat?* rather than, *Do you love eating pumpkin?*

Young children who cannot write may draw three things they like and one thing they don't like. Alternatively, people may move around introducing themselves by saying two things that are true and one that is false. Their partner has to guess which is the false statement.

Feedback: Comment on how participants listened and took turns to share information.

LEARNING NAMES

In a circle each person gives their name proceeded by a positive adjective that begins with the same letter as their name and also

describes something about them. For example, *Sweet Sue*. The next person introduces themselves by saying the first person's adjective and name then their own.

I'm Sweet Sue . . .
Sweet Sue, and I'm Jolly Jenny . . .
Sweet Sue, Jolly Jenny and I'm Kind Kevin . . .

and so on around the group — Kind Kevin, Eager Eleanor, Jolly John, Zealous Zac. After everyone has been introduced with a positive adjective the first person, Sue, says all the names around the group. It is quite difficult to come up with positive adjectives about yourself as we are so used to putting ourselves down.

For young children food is easier to place after their names: Alex — apple, Ivan — ice-cream.

NAME ASSOCIATIONS

To help people remember names, ask them to introduce themselves by stating their name and associating their name with some item they would bring with them on a picnic, for example:

My name is Fred and I'd bring the bread.
My name is Kylie and I'd bring the barbie.
My name is Greg and I'd bring the egg.
My name is Tim and I'd bring the gear to have a swim.
My name is Kay and I'd bring the insect spray.

Alternatively, people can use a rhyme with their name:

I'm Dan the macho man.
I'm Sue with eyes of blue.

(Scannell & Newstrom 1983)

MAKING PAIRS OR GROUPS

CHANGING GROUP MEMBERSHIP

Structuring for collaborative learning by randomly mixing groups not only maximises learning but it enables co-operative skills to be practised. Co-operative skills are learnt and practised by engaging with different people. It is only when you find yourself working with people who do not share similar beliefs and experiences that co-operative skills are necessary for a group to function effectively.

MAXIMISING LEARNING

When we work in randomly selected groups the people with less expertise in the area seek help from those with more skills. There are also benefits for the skilled or gifted student in teaching or making information explicit to other group members. The gifted student may have to find four or five different ways to explain the material. This requires the gifted student to apply the ideas using higher level thinking. As we know, the best way to learn something is to teach it.

A research study by Johnson and Johnson (1989) investigated achievement of gifted, learning-disabled and so-called average students in co-operative learning groups. The results showed that gifted, average and handicapped students achieved more and retained more in co-operative groups than those students working individually. Over 126 research studies support the academic benefits of co-operative learning for children of all ability levels.

RANDOM GROUPING

If we do not randomly select groups the people who look alike or behave the same way choose to work together. The males go together, the females group, people from Cambodia go together, the high achievers move off with other high achievers. Those left — the very shy student, the very bossy student and the handicapped, end up in a group together. These students are at times actively rejected by their peers or neglected.

We do not have to draw so heavily on co-operative skills when we work with people who are like us. Those with less developed social skills tend to be left out with no role models of how to improve on ways to co-operate.

For social equity, that is, gender, race and class equity, random grouping places people together to learn. If we carefully and consciously select groups, the participants may react negatively to suspected social engineering. If groups are mostly random, everyone has a chance to learn from everyone else in the group.

RANDOM GROUPING STRATEGIES

- Place all names in a hat. Each child draws out a name until all have partners.
- Some teachers place the girls' names in one hat and the boys' in the other. A girl selects a name from the boys' hat and in this way pairs of mixed gender are created. This can advantage many boys who have not worked with girls because of peer pressure.
- Number off around the circle 'one, two', 'one, two' to form pairs.
- Work out the number of half the group, say 1–14, and number off to 14. Then all the ones, all the twos, and so on, go together to make pairs.
- For larger groups it is useful to have the same number in each group. The organiser:
  1. Counts the total number of people (N)
  2. Determines the number of people wanted in each group (X)
  3. Divides N by X and has the group count off from one to that number and repeat across the group until everyone has a number.
  4. Asks everyone to go to a table with all the other people with the same number.
- Give a number, picture, shape or a letter to each person by writing it on their name tag. When people make groups, all the number ones, twos and threes make groups, or dogs and horses go together, or A's join together, then the B's, and all the C's.
- Strips of cardboard with co-operative words like interdependence, co-operation or feedback written clearly on one side are cut into three of four pieces. Participants receive one piece of card and find the other parts of the word.
- Number or write a letter on ping-pong balls and toss them to the group with the desired allotment of 1s, 2s, 3s. Then groups are formed with all the 1s together, 2s and so on.
- Assign the names of animals randomly to a large group: dogs, cats, donkeys, elephants, sheep, mice, ducks, and more. The large group, with their eyes closed, makes the sound of that animal and ducks find each other and join hands as do dogs, elephants and so on.
- Blow up different coloured balloons and place a sweet in each before tying the knot. Give out the balloons. Participants form groups according to the colour and shape of the balloon. Burst the balloon and eat the sweet after the co-operative venture.
- Take a pack of playing cards and take out sets of four similar cards to match the number of participants in the group. You may have four kings, four queens, four tens and so on. Shuffle the cards and deal them out. Groups of four are then formed. You could have pairs within the four by having the reds form a pair and the blacks another pair.

- Take the titles of well-known books and write them on cards. Cut the titles into threes or fours depending on how many people you want in each group. Participants match the words in the title. You could photocopy book covers, glue them on card then cut them into as many pieces as you want group members.

- On cards, write the names of three or four book characters from several well-known books. Pin the cards to the backs of participants. As the participant cannot read what is on their back they must ask questions of others. Only *yes* or *no* can be answered. When participants have identified the name of the character, they pair up or group with other characters in the same book. For example, Pooh, Eeyore, Tigger, Christopher Robin.

- Co-operative slogans are written on banners. They are then cut into segments and distributed. People match their segments to create banners. Some slogans are:

  We sink or swim together.
  United we stand, divided we fall.
  One for all and all for one.
  There is strength in numbers.
  The group which plays together stays together.
  No one is as smart as all of us.

- If you don't mind how big the group is, you may randomly assign by calling

  all people with red shoes go together
  all people with brown hair go together
  all people the same height go together
  all people born in the same month go together
  all people who watched the same TV show this week go together
  all people who have read the same books go together

PRUI

This game is pronounced proo-ee. To begin everyone stands in a group and closes their eyes and starts milling around. When you bump into someone shake their hand and ask *Prui?* If the other person asks *Prui?* back then you have not found the Prui. Keeping your eyes closed, find another person to ask.

When everyone is walking around shaking hands saying *Prui?, Prui?, Prui?* the group leader whispers to one of the players that she is the Prui. Since the Prui can see, she opens her eyes. The Prui does not speak, so when someone bumps into her and shakes her hand and says *Prui?*, she says nothing. Players may ask again *Prui?* and if there is no response then this player has found the Prui.

Once you have found the Prui, join hands, open eyes and keep the other hand free to shake hands with someone else searching for the Prui. All members of Prui do not speak yet have their eyes open.

The Prui only has hands free at either end of the line so when people bump into two clasped hands they can feel along until they reach the end of the Prui. Soon everyone is holding hands and a cheer occurs when everyone opens their eyes (Fluegelman 1978).

FARMYARD GROUPS

The children stand in a circle and the teacher whispers the name of an animal to each child. If you want to make six groups then six animal names are whispered quite randomly: duck, pig, horse, chickens, cow and sheep.

When everyone has been allocated an animal, children close their eyes and make the sound of that animal. They move, unable to see, with hands stretched out into the open space to find animals that are the same. Pigs join hands with pigs, cows with cows. Eventually groups of three or four animals are made. These groups then are ready to begin another co-operative activity.

To vary this activity, the names or animals from the Chinese horoscope can be given: rat, ox, snake, boar, monkey and tiger, for example. Young children may have to keep their eyes open to find their group as the animal noises may be too overwhelming for them (Fountain 1990).

GOING DOTTY

Stick small coloured stickers or dots onto each child's forehead. The children have their eyes closed when the sticker is placed on their forehead. If working with a group of thirty, you will need about six colours to make six groups of five.

Once everyone has a sticker eyes are opened. The children make groups based on who has the same colour. There is no talking so all help has to be nonverbal.

This task cannot be completed alone, so children must rely on others to help place them in groups.

Once in groups a further co-operative project can be undertaken (Fountain 1990 and Fluegelman 1978).

WORKING WITH PARTNERS

It is best to begin co-operative learning with partner work. Learning to work with a partner of a different gender, race or ability precedes work in groups of three or four members. Once children can form partners quickly, without put-downs, such as eight-year-old boys grimacing at eight-year-old girls, two sets of pairs can come together to form a group of four. A group of four is the preferred number in a co-operative group. Groups of three can promote partnerships between two people who exclude or talk right through the third person. Foursomes work well on projects where several heads are better than one or two. If the project is a large one groups of four can quickly split into pairs to share the work.

PARTNER OBSERVATIONS

Children quickly find a partner without speaking.
- Observe the partner for 60 seconds.
- Turn back-to-back for 40–60 seconds and change five things about your own appearance.
- Face partner and identify changes.
- Find a new partner.

FINGER DANCING

Form a partnership with someone you do not know very well or someone you have not spent very much time with. Face each other standing a few feet apart. Close your eyes.

Try to use your other senses rather than sight to work out where your partner is. Try to see your partner in your mind's eye. Listen and try to sense where and when your partner moves. Now very slowly lift the index finger of one of your hands and let it move upwards in the air until it comes into contact with your partner's index finger. When this happens, let you fingers stay stuck together.

Let your fingers dance together in ways they want. Try to let them take on a life of their own, sometimes going high and sometimes low. Follow the direction your two fingers take by moving your bodies. Take a step or two if you need to. If you start to lose contact slow down and try to sense where the fingers want to go.

If you are moving around a bit, open your eyes to make sure you don't bump into anyone but don't look at your partner. Sometimes your fingers will stop for a rest and start up again. After stopping twice, open your eyes and tell your partner what you liked about finger dancing.

TRUST FALLS

Partners stand facing each other at double arm's distance. Place hands up in front of your chest. Make eye contact and signal in some way when you are about to lean in and fall onto each other's hands. Once

both are leaning in on each others hands rebound by pushing backwards. Keep your balance then fall again onto each other's hands. Take a step back and fall forward again. The further you step back the harder it gets. To make trust even more difficult stand on one leg. You will have to work hard to keep each other balancing.

TRUST WALK

Pair off and one person plays the role of a blind person by wearing a blindfold or closing their eyes. The other person leads the blind person by the arm and explains where to go by giving directions. After several minutes change over roles.

SHADOWS

Form partners and take turns to lead as person A. Person A may begin moving a small part of their body, such as a finger, and person B, the shadow, makes an exact mirror image by tracing in the air with the same finger. As the 'shadow' gains confidence, large body movements are made and steps taken around the room.

PARTNER INTERVIEWS

Nominate person A and person B. Person A nominates a topic for their personal interview. It could be 'my best attributes', 'sport', 'my childhood memories', 'the future' or 'a fantasy I often dream about'. Person B interviews person A in order to find out more about them as a person.

Person B listens carefully to the responses because they then give a summary of what was said to the whole group at the end of the discussion. After 3 or 4 minutes, tell the group it is time for person A to interview B.

After 3–4 minutes each person briefly describes the content of their interview to the whole group.

Variations: It is best to split a big group of 24 into six smaller groups so that the reporting back on the interview does not take too long.

WHO AM I?

On self-adhesive stickers write the names of animals, machines, or numbers or vocabulary from a theme of study. Young children unable to read will need illustrations. Children have stickers placed on their back. They walk around a space stopping to ask a partner questions. Their partners are only to answer *yes* or *no*.

Young children may require help with framing general questions like *Am I an animal?* to maximise the clues they can receive.

LEARNING PAIRS

This activity illustrates the importance of how information is grouped so it can be learnt easily. The words on sheet A are ungrouped and hard to learn. The group B words are easier to learn.

Form random partnerships. One person takes a copy of the group A word list and the other takes a copy of the group B words. Working individually, try to memorise the names of the twenty common home-related objects in two minutes.

When two minutes are up each person writes down as many items as possible. A minute can be set aside for this.

Which person had most items?

Look at the grouping of items and see if one way of grouping items makes them easier to remember.

Another way of doing this is to divide the large group into A and B. Make pairs and work together learning and writing down the list of words.

Group A:
sofa, dish, bed, sink, car, chair, cup, lamp, towel, rake, desk, fork, dresser, soap, wheel-barrow, mirror, closet, tub, bicycle, coffee table.

Group B:
sofa, chair, desk, coffee table:
dish, sink, cup, fork:
bed, lamp, dresser, closet:
towel, soap, mirror, tub:
car, rake, wheelbarrow, bicycle.

MAKING SPACE FOR OTHERS

In these games and activities participants get up and move around then reform into a circle or semicircle. Sometimes pairs are to move together, sometimes individuals move alone and sometimes the whole group moves.

FRUIT BOWL

All members sit on chairs in a circle. One person without a chair stands in the middle and calls out an instruction. It could be:

All those who had cornflakes for breakfast (or Nutrigrain or Rice Bubbles or whatever) change seats.

All those with freckles change seats.

All those with white shoes change seats.

Once the person in the middle calls the instructions, all participants who fit the description stand up and move quickly to a vacant seat. The person who calls the instruction quickly finds a seat, leaving a new person in the middle.

Rules: You cannot return to your own chair.

You must not sit on the chair immediately to the left or right of your own chair.

You cannot run.

You must not overbalance chairs

ESCAPE FROM THE ZOO

Small cards with a picture or name of an animal are handed out to each person, seated on chairs or the floor, in a circle. Have two or three cards that are the same. The teacher or a nominated participant calls out an animal's name and the animals stand up and run around the circle until they find a vacant space.

The leader calls, *Escape from the zoo*, and everyone stands up and moves to a new position.

A variation of this game is *Rainbow*. Children are assigned colours, either by name or by pieces of coloured paper. The organiser calls red or blue or even two different colours at once. Children run behind the circle to find a space to sit. On the word rainbow, everyone goes to a new seat.

This is a good activity to mix friendship groups and can be used in partner games when people tend to sit next to the same person.

PUNCTUATION CIRCLE

Children often form circles, perhaps to give feedback on how they worked. Hearing feedback from everyone can make us lose concentration so, to keep people moving and the energy up, it is a good idea for the group to change places at given punctuation signals.

The first punctuation mark is to put both fists under your chin once you have had a turn at speaking. This means, *Full stop and the person on my left can go next.*

The next punctuation mark is to put both thumbs under your nose and wiggle all your fingers. This means, *I'm finished but before the next person speaks let's all change places. The person who is on my left after the change will speak next.*

It may be that the person who ends up on your left has already spoken so invent a new punctuation mark to say, *I've already had my turn, and so the next person on my left should go next.*

The game stops when everyone can make the *I've already had a turn* sign.

Feedback is based on how we make space for others and sit next to people we have not sat next to before. It may be useful to limit the changes to after three people have spoken or only to move after people get restless. Physical activity is a great energiser, and renews the attention span and helps us remember material much better than sitting still for a long period of time.

VEGETABLE CHART

Participants are in a circle. Pairs number off 1, 2, 1, 2, and assign themselves the name of a vegetable: broccoli, sprout, pea, bean and so on. The organiser checks to make sure there are no double-ups in vegetable names. The organiser tells the group they are working against time and have five seconds to make the changes.

The first pair calls out the name of a vegetable, say, *asparagus*, and the asparagus pair stands up and quickly exchanges chairs with the first pair. The asparagus pair then calls on another group and exchanges again.

Variation: The group could call *vegetable stew*, and the whole group has to change seats or spaces in the circle.

WORD STORIES

Create a sentence or paragraph based on a topic of interest and write each word on a sticky label.

WE | SAW | KOALA | BEARS, | KANGAROOS, | WOMBATS,
SNAKES | AND | LIZARDS | ON | THE | EXCURSION.
THE | BUS | BROKE | DOWN | ON | THE | WAY | HOME | AND
ANOTHER | BUS | CAME | TO | PICK | US | UP.

The word stories can be played in several ways:

1 The words could be stuck on the back of each member of the class.
2 Groups of five to six students could have several words or part of a phrase stuck to their backs. Without speaking, students create sentences by reading the words on each other's backs and physically moving people around until the sentence is in order.

When the game is over, students can take off the sticky labels and place the sentence on the floor to check that it makes sense.

For very young children the sentence may be written on the blackboard and children match the words from the blackboard to those on their partner's backs. (Rinvolucri 1984)

SAME AND DIFFERENT

Children sit in a circle. One person (Kathy) with a space next to them for someone to sit, starts off by saying:

Kathy: *Bill I'd like you to sit next to me because you've got black hair.*

Bill then says, *Same*, if the feature mentioned, black hair, is the same for Kathy and himself.

The person to the right of the space created when Bill moved says:

Domi: *Sally, I would like you to sit next to me because you have white shoes.*

Sally: *Different.* (Sally has white shoes and Domi has red.)

This game is useful for examining appearances that look the same or different. It also mixes up children who sit only with friends in a circle. (Rinvolucri 1984)

35

COMMUNICATION SKILLS

Effective communication skills are a key to co-operation. In collaborative work, communication involves many skills ranging from more simple skills of turn-taking, eye contact and listening to complex perspective taking, negotiation and conflict resolution skills where many co-operative skills come into play.

Communication involves nonverbal gestures and facial expressions and, particularly, the words we use: the tone, pitch and expression which conveys our knowledge and feelings about the world and our relationships with others.

COMMUNICATING FEELINGS

Schools have traditionally focused on communicating what we *know* and less about how we *feel*. Communicating the feelings that describe whether we feel comfortable or uncomfortable can be especially difficult for boys who, in most western societies, receive covert and open messages, stressing that it is undesirable to display or acknowledge emotion.

The ability to communicate one's emotions may form a basis for the exploration of justice and fair treatment. When words are used to describe what we saw, heard and felt, those who feel mistreated can describe their feelings. Once children have the vocabulary or reference point for describing their feelings they can better relate to and understand the feelings of others who experience injustice.

Competence in speaking and listening is also essential for the prevention and resolution of disputes and conflict. Children who can express feelings and different points of view can call on a range of alternative methods for solving problems. Those who listen carefully and can express their emotions clearly show a greater inclination to give help to someone who is distressed. (Fountain 1990)

EYE CONTACT
WHAT COLOUR ARE YOUR EYES?

Everyone walks around the room until they meet someone they do not know very well. They look at the person's eyes for at least 30 seconds and describe in detail what they saw. It could be the colour like blue or hazel but even more information is called for like the tones, flecks and spots. Once both partners have described their eyes they move on to meet another person they do not know well.

For participants from cultures where eye contact is not common, explain that the activity helps us see and describe each other's eyes and is not intended to be disrespectful.

THE EYES HAVE IT

This activity shows how communication is easier when people have eye contact.

Groups of six are formed and two members of the group sit back-to-back on the floor or on chairs in the centre of the semicircle of people. The group should be able to see both people speak.

Ask one person in the centre to describe something humorous or silly that has happened to them. (For example, a practical joke that was played on them or a silly mistake they made.) As the first person speaks the other listens carefully because they will repeat the message to the group.

Most people will watch the facial expressions, gestures, and nonverbal movements.

Feedback: Ask participants if they heard the same message from both speakers. How were the messages the same or different? How can we make sure our communication is as effective as possible. (Scannell and Newstrom 1983)

THE BONE GAME

This game depends on gesture and can be played by people who do not speak the same language. Versions of this game have been found in many North American Indian tribes. Players have to work out how various bones are being held, so quiet meditation and careful eye contact is needed.

To play you will need four bones small enough to be concealed in closed fists of two players. Two bones are marked with a thread or piece of string tied around them. The other two are left unmarked.

If there are twelve players (a good number) the players sit in two groups of six facing each other. Two people from each group act as hiders at the front of their group. Each group has a set of ten counter sticks. The game is over when one group has taken all the sticks from

the other group.

The two hiders from one group huddle together and plan how they will conceal the bones. They then sit in front of their group with one bone concealed in each hand.

The other group chooses a 'shooter' who will try to guess where the marked bones are.

hiders' group

shooters' group

hiders

shooter

The shooter kneels in front of the hiders and uses a series of hand gestures to indicate the four possible ways in which the bones they hold might be arranged.

The hiders try not to reveal the position of the bones while the shooter looks for any glance or gesture that might give them away. When the shooter feels he knows where the bones are he shouts, *Ho!* and shoots out one of the hand signals. The hiders then open their fists to reveal the bones.

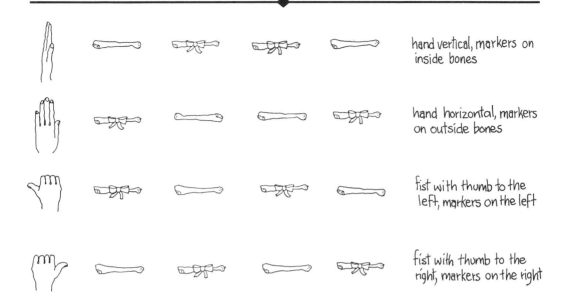

hand vertical, markers on inside bones

hand horizontal, markers on outside bones

fist with thumb to the left, markers on the left

fist with thumb to the right, markers on the right

If the shooter has correctly guessed the position of both marked bones, his group takes the bones and chooses two hiders. The first group chooses a shooter.

If the shooter's guess has missed both bones, he gives up two of his group's counter sticks to the other side and continues shooting. The shooter's signal might locate only one of the marked bones (for example, if the shooter gestures with his thumb to the right and locates only one bone). In this case the shooter takes the one marked bone he has guessed correctly from its hider and forfeits one of his tribe's counter sticks for the incorrect guess. The one remaining marked bone is once again hidden among the two hiders and the shooter guesses again. For each subsequent incorrect guess, the shooter's group must give up another counter stick.

When the shooter succeeds in capturing both marked bones, his group takes a turn at choosing the hiders. The game can go on for ages without the players getting weary. (Fluegelman 1978)

HUNT THE KEY

The players sit in a close circle on the floor. One player is chosen to be the hunter and must sit in the centre of the circle. At first the hunter's eyes are closed while a small object is passed around the circle. When the hunter opens eyes, other players can also pretend to pass the object. When the hunter suspects someone of having the object, he or she calls the name of that person. The passing stops and the person called must reveal whether or not they have the object.

If this player has the object they become the new hunter. If the player has guessed incorrectly, the game continues. (Maguire 1990)

MYSTERY PERSON

All children sit in a circle and one person is sent outside. A chosen child starts an action that changes continually from clicking, clapping, tapping, clapping or a mixture of these and all the others follow suit. The original child comes back in and has to guess who starts the action. The action is changed continuously and eye contact is important in finding out who the initiator of the action is.

After three guesses either replace the starter or choose another child to go outside then return to guess. (Maguire 1990)

LISTENING

Listening is at the heart of communication and co-operation. Interpreting messages depends on the context in which the message was given and the tone, gestures and trust between speakers and listener. *Get real!* could be interpreted as a put-down if there has been past conflict or as a humorous reminder to be realistic or not to take yourself so seriously.

These games and activities can be used for demonstrating how careful listening contributes to communication. The listening for creative visualisation, while an individual activity in itself, may be developed into a group visualisation where the children picture themselves working or experiencing an event together in some way.

SHIPWRECK

One child is chosen to be the ship and the rest are rocks. The rocks sit on the floor and do not move at all during the game. The person who is the ship is blindfolded and must walk from one end of the space to the next without bumping into a rock. When a ship gets too close to a rock the rocks say, *Ssshhh*, similar to the sound of waves on rocks. This warns the ship to steer away carefully. When the ship reaches the shore a new person is chosen to become the ship.

Other hazards can be devised like sharks who give a loud clap as warning.

The feedback can focus on careful listening and ways we help others to avoid the rocks by giving them warnings.

EMPATHETIC LISTENING

Divide the group into groups of three. Assign, or ask the group to assign themselves, roles of:

- speaker: who explains without interruption his or her point of view (two minutes)
- listener: who summarises what is said (approximately one minute)
- referee: who corrects or expands on ideas summarised by the listener

The referee can take notes.

The topic for discussion can be very controversial and taken from current events, school, business or issues of local concern. After all three roles have been played, switch roles and topics if it is necessary. **Feedback:** Were there any barriers to effective listening? Is it difficult to summarise another's comment's? Why?

SYLLABLE CHANT

Participants begin in a circle clapping a regular 4/4 beat. Remind them to keep the beat steady even when chanting. Now the workshop leader says his or her name, *Su-san*, then chooses another name to chant, *Ri-chard*. The words, *Su-san, Ri-chard*, are chanted to fit the beat of the claps made by the group. Richard says his name then follows this with the name of someone else in the group, *Ri-chard, Da-mi-an*. Damian then says, *Da-mi-an, Steph-an-ie*.

This is useful for recognising the stress placed on syllables in words. The beat will speed up so remind participants to slow down the chant to fit the beat rather than quickening the beat to fit the words.

To ensure a gender balance you could ask girls to pick a boy's name and vice versa so that everyone has a turn and is included. **Feedback:** You could comment on how people had to watch and listen closely for their name. Involving and including others is another important idea.

TELEPHONES IN GROUPS

This is usually played in a large group. Try small group telephones with five or six members in the group. In this way all participants can have more frequent turns.

The workshop leader whispers a brief message in the ear of one person in each group: *Friends*, or with more proficient listeners, *Friends can pass on stories*. The groups can have the same message or different messages. It is fun to discuss how the same message can change amongst the group. After the message has been passed around the group ask the last person to say it aloud. Messages can be compared.

Make sure the whispered messages are not overheard.

After working in small groups, bring two smaller groups together. Pass two messages, the same or different, around the circle. Compare what happens to the message in the bigger groups.

Re-form groups to make a circle. Pass a new message around the circle. The message can be about a theme of study or interest.

For a beginning activity, start out with one word until children are proficient. To show children the importance of listening if your first language is not English, a simple word from another language can be passed around. The participants will have more understanding then of children learning English.

Feedback: Comment on the use of careful articulation and slowness of speech so that the listener can grasp the message.

LISTEN AND CLAP

This activity calls for the teacher or more proficient reader to read aloud an extract from a magazine or read a picture book. The reader can quickly skim the book to find words or phrases for the others to listen for. Tell the group the words to listen for and write them on the board so the group does not forget the word as they become engrossed in the story. Children may clap or raise their hands when they hear a chosen word.

Variations of this game can be quite simple recognition of words or even initial sounds in words for young children.

For more mature listeners, propaganda or use of words that people do not understand can be monitored. For example, play through the tape of a political speech and children can clap on the words spoken to raise emotions. To detect difficult, bureaucratic language from government departments, listeners may clap when the hear words that do not make sense or are not understood.

DOGGIE DOGGIE WHERE'S YOUR BONE?

The group sits in a circle and one person is chosen to be Doggie. Doggie leaves the room and the 'bone' is hidden in someone's lap or clothes.

The group then calls, *Doggie, Doggie, where's your bone? Someone has taken it from your home.* As Doggie walks around the circle the class claps quickly when Doggie is close to the bone and slowly when further away.

A variation of this game is the group saying, *Warm* or *Cold* when the Doggie asks questions about where the bone has been hidden.

The feedback stresses participation by everyone and the positive feeling a group achieves from working together.

SOUND CIRCLE

Children sit in a circle and one child makes a sound like a household machine or an animal. The sound is whispered to the next person who passes it on.

This simple game builds up group feelings and careful listening.

COOPER SAYS

This game is a version of Simon Says but instead of being an elimination game the children stay with the group. No one goes out. Cooper can say, *Cooper says everyone shake a person's hand. Cooper says everyone jump.* After five turns Cooper chooses new Cooper, a person who has not yet had a turn.

Feedback can be in the form of attention to active listening and clear expression by Cooper. (Fountain 1990)

WEEKEND LISTENING

Each person writes down ten things he or she does on the weekend, for example Tim may write:

I'm Tim.
I get up late.
I read the cartoons in the paper.
I watch video clips.

Now pair the students and A reads his or her routine to B telling what they do on the weekend. B reads to A who tries to memorise the routine. No more writing takes place.

Now new pairs are made and B takes on A's identity and tells the routine to C. A takes on B's identity and tells the routine to D. The students change partners again, taking on the identity and the routine of the person they have just heard.

Change partners one more time, C takes A's identity to E and D takes B's to F. F and E find the person whose identity they have just heard E finds A (Tim) and tells the routine to the original speaker.

I'm Tim.
I get up late . . .
and so on.

The original speaker compares what was said to the written version.

There is often a gap between the spoken version and the written version so the group may discuss the importance of written information to make a more permanent record. As a listening activity we can point out how information can change from one person to the next. This can be used in conflict resolution activities to show the importance of going back to the source and not just accepting information second or third hand.

WHAT A BORE!

This activity demonstrates how listening changes, depending on whether the information is interesting or boring to participants.

Read aloud a short article (of little interest to the audience) from a newspaper or magazine. When you've finished ask them to write down as many things as they can remember.

Then read an article from an area of great interest to the group — it could be about a favourite book, author or TV show. Ask them to write down as many things as they can remember about the article.

Compare the results.

Feedback: Discuss the importance of sharing information others are interested in. Sometimes we need to need to listen hard to see if the information does really affect us without making quick snap judgements.

CREATIVE VISUALISATION

This is a listening game where children lie flat on the floor with their eyes shut, making no sounds at all. The teacher can ask them to listen for sounds like breathing or heartbeats inside their body. They can imagine the air going in through their nose, into the lungs and out again. They can listen to the breathing of others and see if they can imagine the chest movements of the person next to them as their hearts beat while they breathe. Can they listen for the breathing sounds of a person near them and try to keep in time with the inhaling and exhaling of air.

Alternatively, children can listen for sounds outside their classroom like telephones ringing or cars passing. Images of the people creating the sounds can be formed.

Can you hear people speaking together in the school?

Can you hear a bus moving down the street? Where are the people going? Are they talking together?

Can you hear telephones ring, a radio, TV or another class? What are the people saying?

Picture the people speaking together, listening, taking turns, eye contact, and making facial expressions.

THE SEED VISUALISATION

This is a guided fantasy or guided visualisation activity where children listen to the teacher's voice and create mental images to fit.

Guided visualisation can develop empathy towards others and sensitivity to feelings.

To begin guided fantasies, start with relaxation exercises where each part of the body is tensed then relaxed. Then move to simple creative visualisations like listening to sounds inside your body, then outside. Next children imagine that they are floating in a tank or on a cloud, or being a swarm of bees moving from one flower to the next.

After several introductory sessions, when children find it easy to lie on the floor and picture then describe the images that come to them, longer periods of visualisation can be developed. Take time to let the image develop. Pace the instructions by watching the children engage in the task.

Imagine you are all seeds, beautiful seeds . . .
What colour would you be?
What shape would you be round? square? pointy? . . .
What size would you be?

Now imagine that someone who loves you picks you up in their hand very gently . . . and puts you in a special spot in the ground . . . It's a place that's very soft and warm and safe . . .

Now you're deep in the ground, waiting to grow . . .
The person who loves you comes every day to take care of you . . .
That person gives you water . . . and makes sure no weeds grow around you . . .
You push through the soil.
The sun shines brightly . . .
You grow slowly . . . you form leaves . . .
You grow taller . . . and begin to flower . . .
Open your eyes slowly.
Look around until you see the eyes or someone else you do not know very well . . .
Look at this person and think of them as a beautiful plant that has grown up into the sunlight . . .
Now find someone else you do not know well and sit down with them.

Pairs can be formed, then the pairs form groups of four or six ready to work together.

TAKING TURNS
IMAGINARY BALL TOSS

To encourage turn-taking, participants toss an imaginary ball to each other to give another a turn.

POSITIVE CIRCLE

In the positive circle, each person takes it in turns to provide feedback on how we worked in an activity. Naming it the positive circle stresses the positive nature of feedback which describes what was done well.

Negative examples or criticism are not given as we learn best from positive examples.

MAGIC MICROPHONE

Choose an object that is large enough to be seen clearly but light enough to pass around easily, e.g., a cardboard tube, a block of wood or something similar. The 'microphone' may be decorated with shiny paper and tinsel to make it look magic. When a person holds the microphone they are able to speak. Treat the microphone with respect, sharing it so all have equal air time.

THE MOVER CIRCLE

Children can work in groups of four to six or the whole class can make a circle. There is no touching as all communication is nonverbal. Select music with a clear rhythm as children will create movements to suit the beat. One child, the mover, begins by drawing a shape in the air and this shape is repeated in time to the music. Children in the circle imitate the shape and keep in time with the beat.

When the child who began the rhythmic action decides it is time to change, he or she makes eye contact and nods at another member of the circle. The others in the circle are watching the mover so they catch the nod and eye contact and observer the new mover. The movements continue until most have had a turn.

Try to vary the actions created by the mover by calling *high moves, low moves, medium moves*.

TENNIS STORIES

This game is played in two teams standing opposite each other. A tennis ball is bounced between the teams and as a player takes up the ball they begin a story. When they have told a sentence or two the ball is bounced to another player who continues the story.

It is best to limit the turns to five or so per player so that one or two people don't take over.

BEAN DISCUSSIONS

Have a jar of dried beans and distribute them to each person before the discussion. As each person offers their opinion, they place a bean back in the jar. The discussion continues until all the beans are used up or no one has more to say.

This activity makes children aware of who is doing the talking, and those who speak most of the time become aware of encouraging others to have their say.

Children who are slower at formulating what to say find this game useful as the other children wait for their response rather than doing the work for them. Holding an equal number of beans gives children a tangible symbol that they have as much right as others to participate.

SHOE GAME

This is good for preschoolers in the first hot weeks:
- all children take off shoes and socks at the beginning of a lesson
- line up the shoes and socks like a giant caterpillar
- at the end of the lesson, children silently find their own shoes
- if any shoes are wrong the children can negotiate between themselves, but silently.

TALKING

HOT SEATS

This helps to break down nervousness as people at random are asked to speak for 30 seconds. The topics are written on cards and placed in a hat. Topics include:

- a movie I loved
- a movie I hated
- a dream
- the best thing that ever happened to me
- the worst thing that ever happened to me
- school
- food

Feedback and reflection: How can we prepare ourselves mentally for quick hot seats? Share techniques that others in the group use.

CO-OPERATIVE STORIES

This activity can be a small group or whole class activity. One person begins the story and, after the first sentence, stops and nominates another child to continue. The story can be recorded by the teacher, or someone who writes quickly and legibly, or on tape which can be used in a listening centre.

CLASS WEBS

The children sit or stand in a circle discussing a topic such as 'Food I love'. Have a ball of wool handy. The first person to speak holds the end of the wool. The next person to speak is given the wool (with the first persons still holding the end) and as more and more speak a web of wool is made.

With a simple topic everyone is encouraged to speak. This game reminds children that some people need encouragement from the group to speak. Turn-taking is seen as important.

Variations include wrapping the wool from person to person based on someone who smiled at you today. This gets everyone smiling. Other ideas are to wrap the wool around someone who helped you today or someone you helped today.

EMOTIONS

Brainstorm a list of words to describe feelings and emotions. These words can be use to describe children's feelings and to develop better communication.

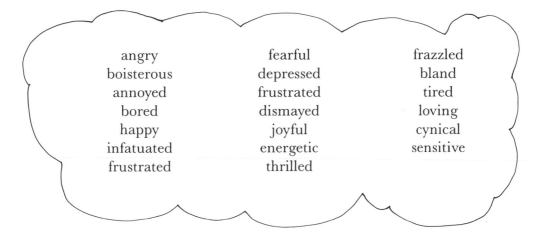

angry	fearful	frazzled
boisterous	depressed	bland
annoyed	frustrated	tired
bored	dismayed	loving
happy	joyful	cynical
infatuated	energetic	sensitive
frustrated	thrilled	

COFFEE POT

This game can be played with any number of players. On person is selected to become 'It'. 'It' selects a verb and writes it down on a piece of paper. Other members of the group ask 'It' questions by substituting verbs in a sentence with 'coffee pot' to try to guess the verb 'It' has in mind. For example, *Do you coffee pot indoors?*. 'It' replies, *No.*

Do you coffee pot in the library? 'It' replies, *No.*

A time limit of two minutes can be set to speed up the game. The last person to ask a question becomes the new 'It' if no answer can be found. (Maguire 1990)

MEMORY TRICKS

Four children are sent outside with a book to read or activity to do. Write down a story on a large chart. The following story is for children in upper primary grades.

> *About 200 years ago in Paris the streets were full of people. They were angry. They broke shop windows and burned down houses. They were rioting.*
>
> *A colonel came into clear a square. His soldiers raised their guns. There was silence. The colonel stood on a wall. 'Ladies and Gentlemen,' he shouted, 'I have orders to fire on the mob. I can see only good, honest people. I want all the good honest people to leave the square, because I want to fire on the mob!'*
>
> *Two minutes later the square was empty.*

One child comes back inside and the story is read out aloud. The student can ask two clarifying questions about the story. Now the first student tells the story to the second student who tells it to the third and so on. Two questions about the story are asked each time.

The rest of the class take notes about how the story is changed each time it is told.

Things added	Things left out	Things changed

After all four students have retold the story in turn, the original written version is read.

COLIN MAILARD

One person elects to be Colin Mailard. Another person is the conductor. The rest of the group sit on chairs in a circle facing inward.

The conductor blindfolds Colin Mailard who then stands in the centre of the circle and the rest of the group quickly change chairs so that Colin Mailard does not know who is sitting where. The conductor indicates when everyone is seated.

Colin Mailard then walks towards the circle helped by directions from the conductor. Upon reaching a player, Colin turns and sits on their knee and has to guess the identity of that player by asking questions. If correct Colin Mailard and the player exchange places and a new conductor is chosen by the old conductor.

If Colin does not solve the mystery of whose knee he or she is sitting on, the conductor can provide clues.

Colin Mailard was a celebrated soldier from Belgium. Though blinded in battle he was a successful soldier and was knighted in the year 999. The king at that time initiated a pageant game that featured a blindfolded knight, from which this version of blindman's buff originated. (Maguire 1990)

SPEAKING IN FRONT OF A GROUP

When children speak in class meetings in front of the whole group the quiet shy children may need support. This support can be in the form of a script or small index cards with ideas listed. It can help if fear of talking in front of large groups, parents, friends and peers is acknowledged and positive strategies are given.

As we all have fears about speaking out in front of a group here are some suggestions for overcoming fear.

1 Use your own style — don't imitate anyone else.
2 Use your own words — don't read.
3 Know your material well.
4 Assume everyone is on your side.
5 Create an informal setting (sit on a table).
6 Practise your presentation — record or video it.
7 Get people involved.
8 Give special emphasis to the first five minutes.
9 Imagine yourself as a good speaker — a self-fulfilling prophesy.
10 Establish your interest in the topic and credibility early.
11 Use eye contact to establish rapport.
12 Show advanced preparation through handouts.
13 Anticipate potential problems and probable responses.
14 Check AV equipment in advance.
15 Obtain information about the group in advance.
16 Convince yourself to relax meditate, self-talk.
17 Prepare an outline and follow it.
18 Manage your appearance — be comfortable and relaxed.
19 Rest up so you are alert.
20 Put yourself in the audience's shoes (They are asking, 'What's in it for me?').
21 Provide an overview of the presentation.
22 Accept some fears as being good — fears can energise us.
23 Identify your fears and categorise them as controllable or uncontrollable and confront them.
24 Practise responses to tough questions or situations.

ELIMINATING PUT-DOWNS

Put-downs can be a habit, a quick reply without thinking or a conscious mean, nasty response. The best way to eliminate put-downs is to make them explicit and this provides all children with the language to describe their feelings of disrespect and harassment or, alternatively, affirmation and build-up.

As adults we can be put down by insensitive gender related comments such as

That was really smart for a girl.
We'd better be careful, the boys are listening.
Tough it out Bob. You are a man you know.
For a clever woman, you're very feminine.

Until these comments are brought out into the open it is hard to be specific about why we feel put down.

PUT-DOWNS

Brainstorm all the mean and nasty words the class can think of and write them on a chart or blackboard.

The group shuts their eyes and the teacher reads the list through. They think about how they would feel to be called such names or have such words said about them.

Follow this up with a session on affirming statements.

AFFIRMING STATEMENTS

Brainstorm all the positive, building up, supportive words you can say about people and their behaviour.

The group shuts their eyes thinks about how the words make then feel. Discuss these feelings.

Put-downs and affirmations lists can be displayed in the classroom to be added to as children hear them in the classroom, playground or at home.

BUILD-UPS

Ask students to write down or draw on small index cards a positive example of 'build-up' behaviour they have seen. The name of the subject may be written on the card or left anonymous.

The build-ups can be placed on a paper ladder on a chart. At the end of several days the card can be taken down and given to the child.

DO SOMETHING GOOD

Make a spinning circle with some of these instruction. The wheel can be rotated and children decide to do one or two of the ideas suggested.

- smile at a stranger
- say hello to someone who may not like you
- do something nice for a younger person
- do something nice for an older person
- help someone you do not know

WORKING AS A
GROUP

Taking on a role in a group helps share leadership roles. This section begins with simple roles and moves to more complex roles. Roles can be:

- observer
- recorder
- summariser
- encourager
- clarifier
- organiser
- time keeper
- and more

CHOOSING THE PERSON TO BE 'IT'

During co-operative games and activities the teacher or facilitator is watchful of who is chosen to start a game, how turns are taken, who is chosen to go on a team, and who is chosen to be 'It' in chasing or team games.

Choosing the person to be 'It' in a game has often been based on eliminating people. The last one chosen is 'It'. The participants may say a rhyme to eliminate members:

My mother said to pick this one
And you are not 'It'.

Sometimes the elimination is based on who is the least agile or who is the slowest runner when children run to a wall or climb a tree calling,

Last one in is a rotten egg,
Last one to the wall is a rotten potato.

Choosing which team goes first, or choosing who will be chosen to go on a team has also been based on elimination; last one chosen is the least desirable team member or last team chosen loses. By varying the way we choose 'It' or who goes first, we can avoid the unfairness and humiliation of the last one chosen. We can say, *Number off when you reach the wall.* Once all have reached the wall say, *The third person to the wall is 'It'.* The first person to touch the wall or the last, could be 'It'. The key idea is to vary the ways 'It' is chosen.

WAYS TO CHOOSE 'IT'

- Pick straws, and the longest straw becomes 'It'.
- Line up in order of height and the third tallest is 'It'.
- Draw strips of paper from a hat. The one with the shortest piece of paper is 'It'.
- Place small pieces of folded paper in a hat. On one piece of paper is a heart symbol denoting 'It'.
- Stand on one leg and the first one to topple over is 'It'.
- Choose from a pack of cards. The highest card is 'It'. Vary this to the lowest number pulled is 'It'.
- Place beans in a jar. Have one bean a different colour. All participants, except one, close eyes and pick beans until the 'It' bean has been chosen.
- Roll one or two dice and the lowest number or highest number is 'It'.
- Line up in order of birthdays. The first birthday in April or last in January is 'It'.
- Use rhymes, but instead of elimination, have the first person chosen as 'It'. Participants hold out a hand to be tapped by the person chanting the rhyme.

Eeny, meeny, miney, mo,
Catch a tiger by the toe,
If he hollers let him go,
Eeny, meeny, miney, mo.

One potato, two potato,
Three potato, four,
Five potato, six potato,
Seven potato more.

Engine, engine number nine.
Going down the Chicago line,
If the train falls off the track,
Do you want your money back?
(Answer: YES)
Y–E–S spells yes and you are 'It'.

The following rhyme invites players to say a number. When this number is counted out the person with the number 5 tapped on their hand (or whatever number is called) is 'It'.

Charlie Chaplin sat on a pin,
How many inches did it go in?
(a guess could be five)
1-2-3-4-5

WHO GOES FIRST?

- Toss a coin and heads you go first.
- Spin a blunt knife and the person it ends up pointing to is first.
- Take a long stick and place hands round it, one after the other. The person whose hands are last on the stick will be first.
- The teacher closes eyes and spins around with one arm outstretched. Whoever she is pointing to when she stops goes first.
- Spin a bottle or a skittle with people in a circle. It points to the person who goes first.

CHOOSING TEAMS

Use the ideas for random grouping to ensure that teams are heterogeneous.

- Have all people with a Sunday, Wednesday or Saturday birthday this year go on one team. Monday, Tuesday and Thursday go on another team. The observers or referees could be the Friday birthdays.
- Names pulled from a hat, numbering off, people with blue eyes go in one team, brown eyes in the other. These are some ideas for randomising team choice so that children work with others with different strengths and abilities.

SENSE ROLES

Assign roles of *ears*, *eyes*, *nose*, and *hand* in groups of four. Gather together a range of objects like a shell, a jar of honey and a clock or watch. You will need about ten to sixteen objects.

The eyes hand out blindfolds to the other three group members. Once blindfolded the eye holds out one object at a time for the ear to listen to, then the hand to feel and finally the nose sniffs it. Once each role has explored the object using only the senses assigned, they describe the object.

Then, as a group, they guess the name of the object.

Discuss the importance of each group member communicating ideas. The importance our senses may be discussed.

RAINSTORM SYMPHONY

The role of conductor is played here. The conductor leads the group just like the conductor of an orchestra.

First, individuals are brought into the symphony by the conductor rubbing his or her hands together and then pointing in turn to

individuals. The conductor swivels around, encouraging all to rub their hands like the conductor did. This sounds like gentle rain.

Slowly the storm gets louder as the conductor introduces a new sound like clicking fingers. Again members of the orchestra join in. Soon hands are clapped for thunder and feet stamped to make the volume increase. There is a huge crescendo of the storm then the volume slowly decreases by clapping, finger clicking and finally rubbing hands together to make gentle rain.

A **variation** of this would involve the whole class divided into groups. One group rubs hands, then next finger clicks and others stamp and clap. The conductor then creates the storm by involving various groups.

SHARING ROLES

This is a very simple game where people mill around, walking in and out and being aware of others' space. Keep on walking until someone yells, *Stop*, at which point everyone freezes exactly where they are until someone says, *Go*. Everyone starts to walk again until *Stop* is called by someone. Anyone can call out either of these two commands at any time.

This activity places the teacher or facilitator as a member of the group freezing or going with others.

Variations include setting a time limit of when to call stop and go. Another variation to give more people a turn is to limit the calls to one per person.

HAGOO

Apparently this game came from the Tlingit Indians of Alaska. *Hagoo* means *come here*.

There are two teams. A chosen person from each team is asked to walk stony-faced between the lines of the two teams standing one metre (three feet) apart.

The two chosen from each team step forward and face each other, bow and walk towards each other, not breaking eye contact until they meet in the centre of the two lines. They are not to laugh or give the smallest smile but must keep walking between the two lines.

The people in the two teams try to do the most outrageous things to get some kind of reaction from the opposing team member who is walking between the lines. They may yell, make disgusting faces, do anything except touch the player.

If a player cracks up, or even gives a tiny giggle or smirk, they join the other team and try to make the opposition laugh.

This game ends when there is only one team left, or when everyone has had a turn down the aisle.

HA, HA, HA

This is similar to Hagoo except the players form a circle. One player begins by saying *Ha*, the next continues with *Ha, Ha*, the next with

◆

Ha, Ha, Ha, and so on around the circle. Each player adds *Ha* to the string of *Ha, Ha's.*

Players are to keep a straight solemn face and avoid laughter. Players who laugh drop out of the circle and form a new circle where they start again with *Ha.*

Another version of this is to have the player that begins to laugh do everything possible to make the remaining players laugh. They can make faces, anything goes except there is no touching or tickling. (Maguire 1990)

GROUP STORIES

In groups assign roles of:

- time keeper
- word checker
- encourager
- ideas person

Write this collection of words on a chart or blackboard:

put	put on	saw
ran	went in	said
went out	ate up	jumped out
walked	put on	ate up
stopped	lay down	heard
picked	came	came in
saw	knocked	lived
asked	said	answered
went in		

Children create a story in groups using the words. These words come from the story of 'Little Red Riding Hood' but encourage a wide range of fables, fairy tales or modern-day stories. When a story has been created and all the words used, break into pairs. Each pair finds a pair from a different group and takes turns to tell the story. Before the stories are told, rub the words off the blackboard to encourage the story to flow. (Rinvolucri 1986)

ROLES WE PLAY

Write up on the blackboard the roles we play in life:

- sister
- friend
- teacher
- cousin
- cook

61

- cleaner
- monitor and so on

In pairs, describe the person you play a role to, for example:

I am sister to my older brother who is 18. My brother works at the supermarket.

(Rinvolucri 1984)

CRIME AND PUNISHMENT

This is a game for upper primary students only.

Form groups of six or role play this in a fishbowl format. Write this on a chart or photocopy for all members of the group to read.

A man got on a train and sat down in a compartment which was empty except for one lady. She took off her gloves. A few hours later the man was arrested by the police. They held him for 24 hours and then were forced to let him go free.

KEY WORDS
30 years
garden
lover
vanish
jail

In groups, assign roles of prosecutor, defence, jury (2), judge, defendant. Only the defence and the defendant have the following explanation for the crime:

Thirty years before, the gloved lady had been married to the man on the train. She and her lover had disappeared and left the country. Before vanishing, they had cut off the two middle fingers of her left hand and buried them in the garden. The police found the fingers while investigating her disappearance and accused the man of murdering his wife and burying her elsewhere. He was jailed for thirty years for a crime he did not commit. He did not recognise her at first on the train. When she took off her glove, he did. He killed her. The police had to release him as he had served his life sentence before committing the crime it was for.

The prosecutor and jury may ask questions of the defence and the defendant who are only to answer *Yes* or *No*. The judge makes sure that all have a turn to speak.

PROBLEM SOLVING

Problem solving as a group involves:

- defining the problem
- brainstorming
- clarifying ideas
- confirming ideas
- elaborating ideas
- seeing consequences
- criticising ideas
- organising information
- finding solutions

INVENTING GAMES

For children who wish to create their own co-operative games there are several principles to keep in mind to avoid team against team or person against person competition.

1 The players may try to defeat a force such as time, gravity or some outside fantasy force rather than their team mates.
2 All players can make their final move at the same time.
3 All players take a turn in sequence and are responsible for one indispensable step towards the final goal.
4 Players combine efforts to reach a set score.

NEW GAMES FROM OLD

Supply game boards from games such as Snakes and Ladders, Monopoly and Trivial Pursuit. Provide cardboard to make cards, dice and counters.

In groups of four players develop a game that is co-operative rather than competitive. The rules for the new game should be written so that the game can be rotated between the groups.

Groups can evaluate the games and give feedback on the clarity of the rules.

FIVE W'S

Newspaper articles about conflict in the world are discussed. Children move into groups of five. An article is read aloud by the teacher, or children read copies of an article or story. Each person then takes on the role of questioner:

- WHO questioner
- WHAT questioner
- WHEN questioner
- WHERE questioner
- WHY questioner

The questioners ask others in the group to answer their question, for example,

> *Who was involved in the riot?*
> *What happened when the people demonstrated?*
> *When did it happen?*
> *Where was the massacre?*
> *Why do you think it happened?*

Each person provides a different response.

This activity will stimulate several rereadings of the newspaper article

64

and a deeper understanding as the children anticipate the questions they will be asked.

PETE AND REPEAT

This is a pair activity to practise clarifying and paraphrasing ideas. Write on the blackboard:

Today is a great day.

Ask two children to sit in the centre of a fishbowl to role play how paraphrasing works. Nominate Pete and Repeat. Pete reads the sentence, then Repeat paraphrases it by saying something like, *We will have a good day today*. Pete says, *OK*, as the paraphrase was fine. Then Pete tells of all the things he has done during the morning. After a minute the teacher may say stop and Repeat paraphrases the information.

The other children can the form pairs and take turns at being Pete and Repeat. (Krieder 1984)

THE MARIENBAD GAME

Write this sentence, or one like it, on the board:

Darling
I love you so much
You must never leave me
If you go, I will die of a broken heart.

Divide the class into two teams. Ask them to reduce the words on the blackboard. They can huddle together to make a decision about which words to delete.

Each team can take turns to delete words from each line, and one or more words can be deleted. Team A goes first and probably deletes Darling. Team B then deletes one word or more from the next line.

The game concludes when as many words as possible are deleted and the message retains as much as possible of the meaning. (Rinvolucri 1986)

CLOZE DICTOGLOSS

Choose a short poem or a short segment of a text to read aloud. Prepare three cloze activities:

1 With all words except the nouns deleted
2 All words except the verbs deleted
3 All words except the pronouns deleted.

Read the text or poem and ask the students to listen and note down all the key words they catch as they listen.

Children then have a few minutes to complete one of the three cloze activities which have been given out at random. Some children will have lists of nouns, others verbs, and the other children will have pronouns. Groups of three are then formed with one member having a list of verbs, another nouns and the third pronouns.

The group of three can share the nouns, verbs and pronouns to recreate the story or poem. When the poem has been recreated children can read it out aloud or check their version against the version written on a chart or the blackboard. (Rinvolucri 1984)

ADD A WORD

Write on the blackboard:

I am a hotel.

Tell the students they can change the meaning of the sentence by adding one word only.

I am not a hotel.
I am a hotel manager.
I am a hotel failure.
I am never a hotel.

Vary the game by changing, rather than adding words. Write up a new sentence:

The wind blew hard.

Students can alter the sentence by changing one, two or more words:

A trumpet blew hard.
A trumpet tooted softly.
Our train tooted softly.

(Rinvolucri 1986)

SENTENCE COLLAGE

Use this activity when the class is discussing the difference in meaning between words, for example 'because' and 'if'.

Construct a set of cards for groups of six to seven students. The cards could contain words from a sentence such as:

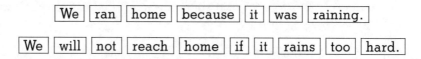

Shuffle the cards and hand them to a group of six students who then lay them out to make a sentence.

The teacher talks to the group about how the sentences were constructed and the meaning of the new words introduced. Homonyms such as there/their, read/reed, heir/air, work well in this activity.

R&R (RESPECT AND RESERVATIONS)

This activity helps children to focus on the problem and not criticise the person. Role play this first with a child and teacher in the centre of a fishbowl. The teacher models how to show respect and reservation:

I like it when you tidy the desk around you but I have reservations about how you put books in the library.

Children may think of family situations and tell the whole group.

I like it when you . . . but I have reservations about the way you . . .

R&R helps place criticism in perspective and is a useful technique for children who may be very harsh and negative critics.

BOB'S GAME

This observation game can be played in the classroom or on a car or bus trip. Rotate turns at playing 'It'. 'It' nominates a direction to look at or an area of the classroom, and a set amount of time is given, say twenty seconds. If travelling along a road, a kilometre or half kilometre is nominated before 'It' says stop.

Once the time is up players look in another direction or straight ahead if travelling. 'It' poses a problem like *How many sparrows were sitting on the telegraph wire?* or *What day does the 12th of July fall on?* The key idea is to ask a question that at least one other person will get correct.

A point is scored by 'It' and the other person(s) if there is agreement, so questions must be posed carefully. 'It' looks carefully at where the other players are observing so that a point can be scored. The object of the game is to have at least one, and preferably more, people agree so that points are scored. If there is a dispute amongst all players no one scores any points. A tricky question in which no one scores defeats the purpose of the game which is to all gain as many points as possible.

HOT AIR BALLOON

Nominate a player to be 'It'. 'It' can be one or two people if the players are mixed ages or involve players who have English as a second language.

'It' chooses a word but does not tell the other players what it is. The players guess the word from clues provided by 'It'. 'It' devises a complicated system of giving clues, perhaps by giving the first letter clue as the first letters in a string of words, for example:

Grandma went for a trip in a hot air balloon and she took a bucket, a blanket and a bun but she didn't take a creamcake.

Players easily guess the first clue is the letter *b*.

The game can be played at this simple level or more complicated rules can be invented by 'It'. For example, the second letter clue could be:

Grandma went for a trip in a hot air balloon and she took a box, a potato and a dog but she didn't take a peanut.

Final clue:

Grandma went for a trip in a hot air balloon and she took a mob, a web, and a cabbage but she didn't take a koala.

The answer is Bob. The second clue is found in the second letter of each word. The third letter clue is the third letter in the list of words.

It is best to start out simply.

STEPHEN'S GAME

This is a much more complicated version of Hot Air Balloon. The game starts with 'It' saying:

I'm going in hot air balloon and I'm taking a sausage. Do you want to come?

The other players can join in by saying, *Yes I want to come.*
'It' replies, *But what will you bring?*
Can I bring a banana?
'It' replies, *No, you can't bring a banana.*
The players have to find out, by a process of elimination, what it is that may be brought.

'It' can give clues like, *You could bring a sandwich but don't bring a bagel.*

The simplest version of this game is to have the objects that can be taken starting with the first letter of the word but if 'It' suggests that this is too easy, second or final letters can be used as clues.

CHARADES

Charades is a team effort based on miming a title of a well-known TV show, book or movie. The team decides on the topic or title, then whether each person will take a word to mime or whether all will mime the words together.

* A beckoning action means that the team mates are getting close.
* A pointing forward gesture means future tense and pointing backwards means past tense.

The audience may call out the answer at any time and, if correct, switch over so the other team has a turn. (Rinvolucri 1984)

LIVING NOUGHTS AND CROSSES

Take nine chairs and arrange them like a noughts and crosses grid.

Form two teams. One team crosses their arms to distinguish themselves from the other team. There is no talking. Members of the teams then take it in turns to sit in a chair, Team 1 (arms folded) then Team 2 (arms down).

The game ends when a team is the first to make a line of team members diagonally, vertically or horizontally across the grid. The teams try to block their opponents, as in traditional noughts and crosses and they have to decide where to sit. (Summerland 1991)

MANAGING DIFFERENCES

When conflict occurs, and the group has to manage differences of opinion without becoming angry and emotional, mediation and negotiation skills are important.

Managing differences involves:

- stating the position or problem
- seeing the problem from another view
- negotiating
- mediating
- reaching consensus

WHAT'S THAT SMELL?

Place cotton wool soaked with various smells like tea tree oil, perfume, sardines, bleach and eucalyptus into numbered containers. Make cards to correspond.

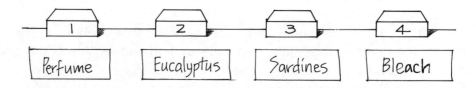

Groups smell the cotton wool. They have to agree on what the smell is and put the appropriate card by the container.

DESERT ISLAND

The group is to go to a desert island to co-operate and learn to live together for two weeks.

The class then divides into groups of four and agrees on ten items, in order, they can take to the desert island. An example of ten items could be: water, book, comb, scissors, radio, tins of food, generator, torch, matches, BBQ.

Remind the class of ways to reach concensus.

Feedback can include a review of the process. What items were easy to agree on?

Variations: Journey to a new planet to set up a colony or go back in history to the year 1700. (Kriedler 1984)

MIXED UP SENTENCES OR SHAPES

In this activity, sentences are cut up into individual words and placed in numbered envelopes. There are five envelopes for each group, so if you are working with a class of twenty-five you will need twenty-five envelopes. If there are twenty-three then still give each group five envelopes.

Envelope 1: sink, the, person, than, Co-operation
Envelope 2: or, Criticise, two, one, saves
Envelope 3: swim, problem, heads, time
Envelope 4: We, not, are, competition, it
Envelope 5: together, the, better, loses

Each group is to construct five sentences without talking, gesturing or signalling in any way. The only way to get a needed word is to have it passed to you by a group member. The sentences when complete can resemble:

We sink or swim together.
Criticise the problem not the person.
Two heads are better than one.
We sink or swim together.
Co-operation saves time, competition loses it.

Feedback can be on how we helped others.

SIX, SIX (OR 66) TECHNIQUE

This can be used in a very large group to discuss issues of concern. People split into groups of six. Each group assigns a recorder. After the issue is chosen, a six-minute period is set aside for the group to talk about it. Tell the group when two minutes are left. Then, with one minute left, tell them to wrap things up. Recorders can verbally report or pin the group's response to charts or walls with masking tape and people mill around to read the responses. (Phillips 1948)

NOMINAL GROUP TECHNIQUE

This is a structured version of small group discussion, and it minimises group domination by one or two people, encourages all to participate and results in a set of solutions or recommendations arranged in order of agreed priority.

1   Divide into groups of five or six people.

2 State the open ended question, *How can we involve parents?*
3 Have each person brainstorm in private all the possible ideas they can generate and jot them down on paper.
4 Have the group members share ideas and record them on a flip chart. One person responds at a time. No criticism is allowed but clarification in response to questions is encouraged.
5 Then each person evaluates the ideas and individually votes for the best one (e.g. the best one gets 5 points the next best 4 and so on).
6 Votes are shared and tabulated. Each group presents a report to the whole class and discussion follows the presentation. (Delbecq & Vande Ven 1971)

BRAINSTORMING

1 No critical judgement is allowed.
2 Freewheeling is allowed; the wilder the ideas the better.
3 Quantity not quality is desired.
4 You are seeking the combining and linking of ideas.

Introduce the basic rules and explain that too often we knock ideas on the head by saying, *We tried it last year* or *We've always done it that way*. In groups of 4–6 give 60 seconds to come up with all the different uses there could be for a paper clip. Remind participants that crazy ideas can often be the best.

POSTER CHOICE

This activity also works well as a getting acquainted activity. The organiser sets up a display of posters, cartoons or magazine pictures. Each person selects three items from the display. The criteria for selection could be the 'most relevant to you', 'most interesting' or 'most striking', whatever the organiser suggests. Each individual has a first, second and third preference.

The next stage is for each participant to find a partner. The two explain their choices to each other. Then, as a pair, they agree on three out of the six items they find the most appealing or interesting. Next, each pair meets up with another pair and the process is repeated. The four people have to come up with three items agreed between the four of them.

To continue the selection process pairs may continue to meet new pairs until the whole group can make a final selection on their preferences. If there are more than twenty people in the group it is possible to photocopy the display of posters, cartoons or pictures and find out if each group selects the same items as their first preference.

SOCKS

Tell the children that on the bus/train you saw two young men. One was wearing white socks and the other was wearing black socks. Suddenly they exchanged one of their socks. They got off the train wearing one black and one white sock each.

Students brainstorm independently and write down reasons why this happened. The men exchanged socks:

> . . . *in order to* . . .
> . . . *because* . . .
> . . . *as a* . . .

When about five reasons have been written, form fours and decide on the three best hypotheses. Each foursome then writes the best three hypotheses on the blackboard.

Consensus on one best reason can be reached by counting the number of similar reasons various groups came up with, or by voting on the best reason as a whole class. (Rinvolucri 1984)

COMING TO CONSENSUS

1   To start out you can write 'consensus' on the blackboard and explain that consensus is when a group comes to a decision that is acceptable to everyone, even if it is not everyone's first choice.
2   With the whole class involved, brainstorm a list of trips or excursions people would like to take.
3   Each person selects one trip and writes it down on paper.
4   Groups of three then share ideas and brainstorm four trips they would all like to take.
5   Now form larger groups of six. These larger groups come up with two trips that each person would like to take.
6   The groups of six then report to the whole class. Combine the lists and have the whole group come up with one trip all would like to take.

Feedback at the end of this activity can involve people reflecting on the steps they took to solve the problem. The steps for social problem solving may be considered:

• What is the problem? Deciding on a trip.
• Alternative solutions? Brainstorm alternatives.
• Consequences of the alternatives? List the disadvantages/advantages of each.
• Reach consensus? Reach consensus through discussion and as a last resort take a vote.

(Kriedler 1984)

GAMES FOR BIG SPACES

These activities require a big space to encourage movement.

PEOPLE OF THE MOUNTAIN

This is a co-operative version of 'I'm the king of the castle' where one person tries to get to the top of something at the expense of others.

The aim of this game is to get everyone on top of a hill, chair or crate without people falling off. (Kriedler 1984)

MUSICAL LAPS

At the start, each person has a chair to sit on. Music is played and children stand and move around the space. The teacher removes one chair and the music stops. Children then sit down on the nearest chair. As one chair has been removed the children without a chair will have to sit on each other's lap. The music starts again and another chair is removed.

At the conclusion of the game everyone is sitting on one person's lap. No one is left out and children have to work out ways to include others and hold them up so nobody falls on the ground.

MUSICAL HUGS

This game requires music that is played for a short time then switched off. When the music stops everyone must hug someone near them. When the music starts up again they move as partners to make a foursome next time the music stops. This goes on with everyone finding a new partner until the whole group is joined.

A variation of this is to have the teacher or a child call out a number and children make a group according to the specified number.
Feedback: Children may not be used to physical closeness with others so feedback can focus on the fact that we feel better after a hug. Giving someone else a hug is a good feeling.

CO-OPERATIVE MUSICAL HOOPS

Two children move along inside one hoop. When the music stops they form a foursome with another group and place the two hoops together. The music starts again and children move. More are added to the hoop until the hoop can hold no more.

A variation of this is to begin with a hoop for each child on the floor. Children hop, run or skip to the music but when it stops children move to stand inside a hoop. The teacher removes a hoop each time so more and more children have to stand together inside a hoop. Again physical contact and co-operation is essential. (Fountain 1990)

CROWNS AND STATUES

Each person is given a beanbag to balance on their head. They then move around to music. If a beanbag falls off, that child becomes a statue and cannot move until another child comes along and replaces the beanbag on top of the statue's head.

For very young children working in pairs may be a good idea as they can then watch and help each other. Another variation is for one pair to sit in a wide circle watching their partner who walks around inside the wide circle. If the partner's beanbag falls off the partner in the circle replaces it for the statue. The partners should switch roles every few minutes. (Fountain 1990)

75

BUMP

You need music which can be turned on and off as people walk around the room. When the music starts, all players walk around in all direction, deliberately bumping gently into as many people as possible. When the music stops each player stops and links arms with their nearest neighbour, exchanging names. When the music starts again, the players remain in linked pairs, this time avoiding bumps while talking to their partners.

The music stops and each player grabs another person who links arms and introduces themselves. Groups can get bigger and bigger.

With younger children, each time the music stops they can form a different pair and follow one set of instructions such as shake your partner's hand, walk backwards together, hug each other and so on. (Pax Christi 1980)

CARS AND DRIVERS

In pairs, in a big space, children decide who will be the driver and who will be the car. The car keeps its eyes shut through the whole process. The driver stands behind the car with eyes open and hands resting gently on the car's shoulders. The driver may vary speed and turn stop and start again.

This activity is best done nonverbally so gentle touch is the way of communicating.

Feedback can deal with trust and ways of communicating to others who may not have full sight or hearing. (Fountain 1990)

CATCH THE DRAGON'S TAIL

About eight to ten people line up, one behind the other, to make a dragon. Arms are placed around the waist of the person in front. The last person to line up tucks a scarf or handkerchief in the back of their belt. At a given signal the dragon begins to chase his or her tail. The person at the head of the dragon tries to snatch the handkerchief by chasing round and round in circles. People have to co-operate for the dragon to stick together. Those in the middle have to pay close attention to know which way to turn.

Once the head captures the tail the head puts the handkerchief in his or her belt and becomes the new tail. The second in line then becomes the head of the dragon.

Another version is two or more dragons trying to catch each other's tails.

NO HANDS

Form pairs then take one object like a beanbag or a cushion. The pairs walk around the room balancing the object between them. The object could be balanced between elbows, knees, heads or backs. After 30 seconds, change the positions of the object. If elbows balanced the bean bag then switch to heads or knees.

HUG TAG

This is like the usual chasey games except the only time a player is safe is when they are hugging someone else. (Fluegelman 1976)

PEOPLE PYRAMIDS

These pyramids are made of people. Start with four strong bodies for a base. Then add three middle-sized stable people. Next, two courageous bodies and last of all the lightest most agile person in the group.

The big rock candy mountain is a more ambitious pyramid and has a circular base with up to ten people. It is possible to go higher than four levels, say to five or six.

SIAMESE SOCCER

This is a lot like soccer except players are in pairs with their ankles tied together in three-legged-race fashion. The ball can be kicked with the 'big' foot or the free foot. The goalie can be made up of two people tied back to back.

You set the game up for soccer with boundaries, goals and, of course, teams. Mix up the pairs so that big and small, heavy and light players have to consider each other as well as kicking the ball.

To break down the traditional two team idea it is possible to have three teams or even four.

CATERPILLAR

Everyone lies down side by side on the grass or carpet in a long line. Try not to have any space at all between each body. The person at the end of the line rolls over on top of all the bodies until she gets to the end of the line then the person at the other end starts rolling. Two or three teams of caterpillars can operate if there is a big group.

KNOTS

This game is best played with a group of 5–7 people. As the group becomes more proficient, more can be added to make groups of 12 or even a whole class group of 30.

All stand close together shoulder to shoulder and place hands in the centre. Everyone grabs the hands of two different people. It works best if you don't grab the hands of the person directly next to you. Now unravel the knot. As you are all in it together it helps if you think about ways to unravel the knot and to talk about it rather than everyone tugging, pulling and going in separate ways.

When the knot is unravelled you will find yourself in one large circle or, occasionally, two interconnecting ones.

If the knot is just too hard to unravel you can have an emergency break in hands to fix the problem. (Fluegelman 1978)

STAND UPS

This co-operative game begins with two people standing back-to-back. They slowly lower themselves to the ground with knees bent but elbows linked for balance. With practice and co-operation between both bodies it is possible to balance even if partners are of different weight and size.

Now groups of three and all stand back-to-back and slowly ease themselves down to a sitting position and up again. Make a group of four or even five. See how many people can join the group and still be able to stand up without falling over.

ROPES

The whole class makes a line holding hands with the person on the right. Without breaking this line the whole line moves under the arm of the person on the left-hand end of the line. When everyone has gone under the arm the line is reversed.

BRITISH BULLDOG

This game can be played by all ages. With a large group of people (20 or so) choose two people to go into the centre and the others go to two end zones. When the people in the middle call out, *British Bulldog 1-2-3!* the other players try to run past them to opposite ends of the field without getting caught.

If a person is caught they are held up in the air with their feet off the ground, long enough for the catcher to say, *British Bulldog 1-2-3!* Anyone who is hoisted into the air then joins the catchers and stays in the middle.

Catchers have to be gentle. The runner you catch does become your team mate so don't squeeze the breath out of them and when caught try not to struggle too hard.

Co-operative lifting is needed with very heavy people. Two or three people may life a very hefty player.

The game ends when there is no one left to catch. (Fluegelman 1978)

BLOB

The Blob is an outer-space monster that swallows people. This game starts out like chasey or tag but instead of an individual catcher there is a group catcher. When the first catcher catches someone she joins hands with him and he becomes part of the Blob.

The Blob is quick moving and can break into sections to catch people. It can trap people in a corner and break into parts if it looks as if its prey is escaping. The game ends when everyone is a part of the Blob. The last person caught becomes the new Blob for the next game. (Fluegelman 1978)

ROCK/PAPER/SCISSORS

This is a version of the old game where partners make various fist shapes to try to outwit each other.

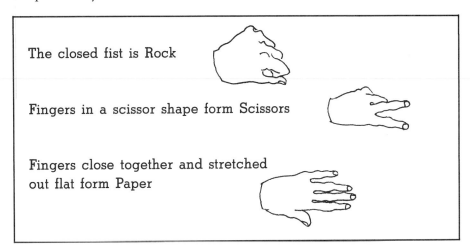

The closed fist is Rock

Fingers in a scissor shape form Scissors

Fingers close together and stretched out flat form Paper

The pecking order is:

- Paper covers Rock
- Rock breaks Scissors
- Scissors cut Paper

You will need two teams. There is a centre-line over which the teams meet. There is also a free zone for people to run to.

Each team huddles and decides on a symbol to use to outwit the other team. Once a symbol is decided the two lines or teams face each other and chant three times:

Rock/paper/scissors
Rock/paper/scissors
Rock/paper/scissors

and as a big group they simultaneously call their agreed word and make the symbol with their fists. The team with the winning symbol chases the other team, trying to tag as many people as possible before they reach their free zone.

In case both teams decide to chant the same thing it is a good idea to have another symbol stored up to use as an alternative. If this happens, begin chanting again,

Rock/paper/scissors,
Rock/paper/scissors,
Rock/paper/scissors,

and call and make the new symbol.

Players who are caught join the team of those who caught them. In this way, teams constantly change numbers and the game keeps going with no one eliminated.

The inventors of this game bet that if you find yourself as a one-person team against twenty-nine others the other team will call Rock if you call Paper. (Fluegelman 1978)

NEW VOLLEYBALL

Here are several versions of volleyball that do not emphasise competition. (Fluegelman 1978)

Rotation volleyball

Number the players 1-9 and after each team has served, players rotate to the other side. This changes the emphasis from playing to win to playing to enjoy the game for itself. To score you have to play your hardest no matter whose side you are on.

Volley-volleyball

This version changes the scoring system. A team can score up to three points if three team members touch the ball before it goes over the net. If only one person hits the ball then one point is scored. This prevents ball hogging as people push the ball to other team members before it sails over the net. A game is 35 points.

Volley-volley-volley-volleyball

This is a version of Volley-Volleyball. Every team member must touch the ball at least once before it goes over the net. This game works best if there are not too many members of a team. Everyone gets a chance to join in. Keep the scoring low for a game — say nine points.

SKIN THE SNAKE

Players need to wear trousers or shorts for this game. The best way to learn how to play the game is to do it until it feels right. Each team has about twelve players lined up one behind the other.

Reach between your legs with your left hand and grab the right hand of the person behind you. The person in front of you is reaching back to grab your right hand. Once hands are held you have a chain. At a given signal the person last in line lies down on the ground on their back. It is easier if people are very tightly bunched together. The person in front straddles her body and lies down on his or her back right behind the first person.

All players on the ground must continue to still hold hands. The game starts again after everyone has had a turn of lying flat on the ground. To begin again the last person to lie down stands up and walks forward pulling everyone up as they go.

When the last person is standing up you have put the skin back on the snake and run as a team, still holding hands, to cross a finishing line. If anyone breaks hands during any part of the process you must stop, go back to that point and reconnect before proceeding. (Fluegelman 1978)

BUG TUG

Start out doing this in twos. Draw a line or place a streamer or rope on the ground. Have partners standing back-to-back over the line. Both people then bend over and reach between their legs and grasp each other's wrists. Now start tugging and see who gets pulled over the line first.

A **variation** of this can be played with a large group. With a large group, stand in lines of about ten people with everyone back-to-back. One line takes a small step to the right so that the person behind you is a little to the left or right. Everyone bends down and crosses their arms between their legs. They should come across the hand of a person on their left and the person on their right. Everyone should have the hands of two people except those on the end of the lines.

See if, as a group, you can walk in various directions. Say, *Walk toward the tree*, or *Walk towards the flag pole*, or *Walk towards the gate*. (Fluegelman 1978)

OOOH-AAAH

Start with everyone in a circle joining hands. A person nominated starts out by giving a squeeze handshake to the person on their right. This gets passed on to the next person and soon you get the original message back. Now start off another message where you say *Ooooh* to the person on your right. Send another *Aaah* message on your right. These Ooohs and Aaahs will travel around the circle and one person will get both at once.

Variation: You can change the directions of the ooohs and aaahs by saying them back to the person who gave them to you. Add more sounds or squeezes to keep the game going.

AMOEBA RACE

To become an amoeba you need about four people as protoplasm and six or so as the cell wall. The cell wall surrounds the protoplasm by joining hands and facing outward. A nucleus is the person who instructs the group on what direction to take as the amoeba moves.

Try walking around outside and even walking around the block. You may have teams of amoeba walking towards specified objects.

CAR WASH

Groups of about 8 or 9 stand in two lines facing each other. One person at the head of the line is moved through the car wash, pushed gently along by the remaining people in the line who give words of encouragement to this person. Then the next person goes through the car wash until everyone has had a turn.

SPIRALS

Everyone joins hands and makes a big circle, then one person drops hands and moves around to make a spiral. The other person with a broken hand clasp stays put and a spiral is created around him or her.

Once a spiral is created stay still and tight to feel the group energy. The group may cheer or yell or sway together.

To unfold the spiral still holding hands, the person in the middle ducks down and crawls out through people's legs. The whole group follows as the spiral magically uncoils.

THE LAP GAME

The group stands one behind the other in a circle and everyone slowly sits down on the lap of the person behind them. To work well, this has to be done carefully. When you are sitting on the lap of the person behind you, you can lift you right hand and still keep balance.

There is no tickling or giggling as soon as one person giggles the circle will fall in.

Apparently this game originated with Empress Eugenie, who told the story of how her soldiers kept dry while resting in the wet field.

The record for lap sitting is a group or 1468 students in Palos Verdes in California. A group of 1306 sat on each other's laps in New Zealand. If you want to break these records, make sure the participants sit on each other's laps and not just knees.

ALPHABET STATUES

Working in groups of 4–6, children form letters of the alphabet or numbers. When a letter or number is called, the group must negotiate how best to arrange themselves to make the letter. It is wise to warn children to include others so that everyone's suggestions are taken into account.

RUNNING THE GAUNTLET

Participants line up in two lines facing forward. Each participant lifts their arm to a horizontal position to create a barrier. One student stands at one end of the line and runs through the two lines at top speed. As they run, each person in line must drop their arm to allow the person to pass.

(Summerland Education Resource Centre 1991)

CLASS SCULPTURE

A group of thirty or so sit in a circle. The aim of the activity is to create a giant sculpture of a machine of some kind.

1 A volunteer strikes a pose in the middle of the floor.
2 Each person joins on to the sculpture.
3 When everyone is attached they stay like this for a minute or so.
4 Everyone then leaves the sculpture in the order they went in.

All this is done in silence.

NEWSPAPER SQUEEZE

Try to fit as many people as possible onto one piece of newspaper. Participants will have to be creative about holding on to each other. You may decide to have each person stand on a tiny piece of newspaper or piggyback on each other so that all, or as many as possible fit on the paper.

BODY PARTS

Form small groups of 4 or 5 people. Have the group place hands or feet on the floor but explain that the body parts that touch the floor are limited, for example only three feet and three hands.

This means that the group members have to work out ways of supporting each other on only three feet and three hands.

Modify the number of body parts to suit the age of the participants as younger children may find this activity more difficult than older children who have a greater sense of balance.

GROUP KNOTS

Participants sit in a circle and are given a letter A, B or C.
Step one: Those with A cards move to the centre of the fishbowl. One person from group A is asked to leave the room. The rest form a circle holding hands.
Step two: Without letting hands go, Group A tangles up into a knot.
Step three: The person from outside comes back and untangles the knot, giving instructions about who should move where.

Groups B and C provide **feedback** on how the group members helped each other. (Summerland Education Resource Centre 1991)

SHARKS

Place children in groups of 4–6. Each group has a sheet of newspaper. Groups dance around their 'island' until the music stops. When this happens everyone has to move on to the island. If any person has any part of their body touching the floor rather than the paper the whole group is eaten by sharks.

Then newspaper is folded in half and the game begins again.

SHARKS AND ISLANDS

This is another version of *Sharks*. A number of hoops are placed on the floor. Participants move in and out of the hoops and, on a given signal, jump onto an 'island'. As the game progresses hoops are removed one by one so that more people have to fit onto each island.

The idea of the game is to try to hold each other on so that no one falls into the water and gets eaten by the sharks. This gets quite difficult when there is only one island left. (Summerland Education Resource Centre 1991)

PART THREE

CO-OPERATIVE
LEARNING IN ACTION

CO-OPERATIVE RESEARCH PROJECTS

Co-operative research projects involve problem solving, managing differences and reaching decisions about ways to research and work together. Co-operative skills are necessary whether the research projects are small or large, ranging from finding out about the life cycle of a frog to how a hospital works.

Projects allow participants to interact, learning is active rather than passive and, because research projects are drawn from children's interests and familiar environments, the knowledge acquired has relevance for the learner.

Co-operative research projects lead children to acquire knowledge in areas that interest them. While the teacher may help children frame their research questions, the project topic must come from the children's interests in order to maintain their enthusiasm. Katz and Chard (1989) state:

> Project work takes into account the acquisition of knowledge, skills, dispositions and feelings. It can provide learning situations in which context and context-enriched interactions can occur about matters familiar to the children. Project work can provide activities in which children of many different ability levels can contribute to the ongoing life and work of the group. (p. 42)

According to Katz and Chard, the following research projects can be undertaken by young children.

RESEARCH PROJECT TOPICS FOR YOUNG PEOPLE

1 Finding out about the participants themselves: homes, babies, families, favourite food, TV shows, toys, games
2 Exploring the local community: people, hospital, shops, building site, transport services, fish market and food market
3 Investigating local events and current affairs: annual fairs, shows, important anniversaries, royal weddings, independence day, a visit by a famous person.
4 Exploring place: neighbourhood, roads, directions, landmarks, rivers, hills, woods, transport.
5 What is time? How is it measured? Clocks, seasons, calendars, festivals, holidays, historical objects, historical events.
6 Exploring natural phenomena: weather, water, wind and air, plants, animals, mini beasts, rocks, sea, dinosaurs.
7 Investigating concepts such as: opposites, patterns, colour, symmetry.

8 General knowledge: deserts, ships and other vehicles, inventions, space travel, rivers

9 Miscellaneous research projects: hats, black holes, puppets, bookweek

PLANNING FOR CO-OPERATIVE PROJECTS

When planning any co-operative research project the following co-operative learning principles can be present:

- shared goals
- positive interdependence
- mixed ability groups
- shared leadership
- frequently changing group membership
- group and individual responsibility
- use of co-operative skills
- group reflection and feedback

The example below illustrates how a teacher created a co-operative garden.

COMMON GOALS

When planning a garden, agreeing on a common goal is the starting point. Not all children may be interested in a vegetable garden, some will want flowers. In fact even the vegetable growers will want different vegetables. The important goal to clarify is, *Do we want a garden?* If yes, then what goes in the garden is negotiated with give and take on all sides so that everyone remains committed to the project and feels involved and included.

The key goal to agree on is that the group wants to put time and energy into making a garden and not an adventure playground or a something totally different.

POSITIVE INTERDEPENDENCE

Next, positive interdependence calls for skill in structuring the project so that the roles of the participants are interdependent. Perhaps the creation of the garden involves creating small sub-tasks for various groups.

MIXED ABILITY GROUPS

Rather than twenty or thirty children working as one group, it is best to randomly divide the large group into subgroups. Numbering off or mixing up by pulling names from a hat works well. Now there are many small groups with roles randomly assigned. Each group is responsible for developing a section of the garden. There is individual accountability built in too.

SHARED LEADERSHIP

One child could be designated as an overall organiser, another as financial controller, quality checker, the tidier could collect and put away materials used by the group.

FREQUENTLY CHANGING GROUP MEMBERSHIP

If groups are changed regularly, children have the opportunity to work with many different people. The teacher's role is to observe the children working together and orchestrate new groupings when tasks are completed.

GROUP AND INDIVIDUAL ACCOUNTABILITY

Individual accountability is planned by assigning roles so that everyone has a part to play. Each team member can report to the whole group on what they achieved and how they worked.

> *As an organiser I did . . .*
> *As a quality checker I . . .*
> *As a financial controller I . . .*
> *As a tidier I . . .*

A diary or journal recording what was done can help to ensure that there is no freeloading by individuals. Finally, individuals can suggest ways to improve they way they worked for next time.

CO-OPERATIVE SKILLS

Co-operative skills which focus on communication, like turn-taking, listening, one person speaks, and no put-downs, are part of effective project work. So too are the more complex skills of problem solving, negotiation and mediation. Several of these skills, for example, criticising ideas not people and problem solving strategies can be taught by making them explicit and giving time to practise them. Feedback and reflection on how the team worked places co-operative skills high on the team's priorities. Working effectively with others gets the project done more efficiently in the long run.

FEEDBACK

Feedback and reflection about how we work with others can occur at the end of each session in order to frame goals for work the next day or in the next session. Setting aside time for feedback is important. Feedback can be the most powerful learning experience because team members reflect on how individuals worked or how the group worked. This centres the group once more on the co-operative nature of the project and inspires and creates energy to go on and improve.

THE TEACHER'S ROLE

Flexibility is the key to organising co-operative research projects. In some projects, clearly defined roles will be important. At other times children will not need to use roles. Sometimes children will work as individuals gathering resources to share with their group. Sometimes friends will work together and at other times children will work with those they do not know well.

Vary the co-operative structure to suit how the group is working. For example, if the group is not taking turns introduce a structure so that turn-taking is built into the activity.

For example, a class of six- and seven-year-olds visited a garden centre. When they came back to the classroom they discussed what they saw and decided to make a group frieze. A two-metre square of paper and pots of paint were provided. There were three co-operative instructions given.

1   Three children only are to paint at a time.
2   Each child is to paint only one or two items.
3   After a set amount of painting time, each child is to give a turn to another child who has not had a turn.

As the painting continued some of the items became smaller because the space filled up, but most of the items were included. The only suggestion made by the teacher was that the white spaces left over could be filled with a yellow wash. (Katz & Chard 1989)

The teacher orchestrates the learning and shapes the overall outcome of the project. Each teacher's enthusiasm, ability to gather resources, and to clarify and confirm what has been learnt are steps along the way towards completing the project.

CASE STUDY

Older children benefit enormously from co-operative research projects. The eleven-year-old students in Jane O'Loughlin's class were fascinated by what was happening the Middle East Gulf crisis. They had many good, probing questions. Why was the Gulf War happening? What religious groups were in the area? What is Islam? What is Judaism? How does Christianity differ from these religions?

The class, with Jane, decided to set up a research project to explore several religious beliefs operating in the Middle East. This research fitted into the social education and religious education curriculum set by the school. World religions was a topic of study so Jane was pleased when the children's interests so neatly dovetailed into the suggested curriculum.

There were many ways to go forward from here to plan for children's learning. Jane could do the research herself and offer distilled versions of information or facts for the class to rewrite as individual projects; she could ask the class to form friendship groups and complete group projects on religions of the Middle East. She chose to structure the children's learning around co-operative learning.

Jane decided to use two ideas to build success in learning into the program:

- demonstrate and make explicit each step of the research process for working in projects
- demonstrate and make explicit co-operative learning skills

SESSION 1: GOALS AND GROUPS

Jane, after careful thought, came up with a goal which allowed for great diversity in content and format and was broad enough to suit each student. The students knew that a product was due at the end of term but the form it could take was open.

> Your group task is to produce a fact booklet on one of the major religions of the Middle East to be photocopied and shared with others.

Jane listed learning goals for the class so that she could assess the effectiveness of the research project as well as the children's own learning. These learning goals concerned students' knowledge of the religions of the Middle East, understanding of the research process, plus use of the co-operative skills of working together

THE RESEARCH PROCESS

The students listed preferences in order of which religions they would like to study. They listed first, second and third preferences and Islam, Judaism or Christianity showed up as the three main choices.

Jane decided to randomly group students in groups of six so she took squares of coloured cardboard and cut them to make six-piece jigsaws. Students withdrew a piece of jigsaw from a hat and found other members to complete the jigsaw square.

To make sure there was a gender balance in the groups she intervened when three girls or three boys had selected a particular coloured card. She said, *Now it's time for boys to choose reds or green because we have three girls with this colour.* Children with mixed ability were randomly assigned to groups and only the gender mix required intervention. Her work in co-operative learning had alerted her to difficulties experienced in groups where the number of boys or girls was too uneven.

After the groups had been formed, Jane showed how to list the information already known as a way to generate questions to pursue in research. She wrote two headings and columns on the blackboard:

What we know	What we need to know
Christianity has holy trinity	Is Jesus a prophet?
Jesus was resurrected	How did it start?

She worked with the class brainstorming what was known about Christianity then building lists of questions to guide the research. Next a list of key words was made by highlighting or underlining major words in the column, *What we need to know.* These key words were then made into research questions in order to gather relevant information.

CO-OPERATIVE SKILLS

To remind the group of the importance of listening to each other Jane asked the class to make a large circle or fishbowl. A group of four articulate children who also could listen well went into the centre of the fishbowl to discuss the question, *Is religion important in our life?* The topic was relevant to the research but the focus for the class was how did the small group listen, take turns and encourage each other to take turns.

The class then built up a Y chart to describe listening behaviour.

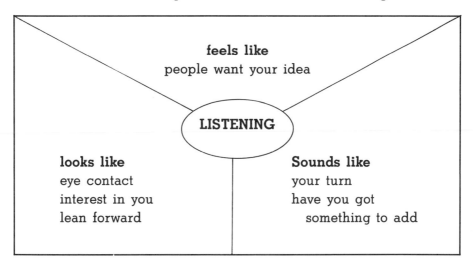

In later sessions, over the next ten weeks, co-operative skills such as turn-taking, clarifying, summarising ideas, negotiating and taking responsibility both as a group and as individuals were role played by members of the class. This made the co-operative skills explicit and focused the students on ways in which we co-operate and work together.

The students nominated co-operative roles to play in the session. They had been introduced to group roles during the year and selected some of these roles to play.

- recorder
- time keeper
- reporter
- clarifier
- summariser

SESSION 2: ORGANISATION OF TIME

RESEARCH

There were ten weeks set aside for the research project. In the second session a time line for the number of weeks and checkpoints for the research process was drawn up by the class.

group to set dates

| note taking | progress meetings | draft 1 | progress meetings | draft 2 |

Each group set dates for progress meetings at least once each fortnight and booked time to conference with Jane about their drafts.

SESSION 3: FINDING AND SHARING RESOURCES

Once the roles for each group member were finalised and the research questions listed, the groups mostly decided to work in pairs to research the information. The groups brainstormed where resources could be found

- libraries
- kids themselves — Maronite Christian and Greek Orthodox child in the class
- AV resources
- priests

SESSION 4–8: PROGRESS MEETINGS

For each progress meeting the group drew up an agenda and organised members to play the co-operative roles of convener, minute keeper, time keeper, organiser and collator of papers.

In each meeting, research skills and co-operative skills were demonstrated and practised. For example, in session 4, Jane modelled how to keep track of a bibliography, ways to skim and scan texts and how to take notes. She also played a listening game to practise the co-operative skills needed to ensure that everyone's ideas are considered.

SESSION 9: ORGANISING AND PRESENTING INFORMATION

Jane modelled how to organise information and suggested ways the research could be presented. Graphic organisers like schematic webs and time lines were presented.

beliefs   symbols
(Islam)
ceremonies   key people

beliefs   symbols
(Judasim)
ceremonies   key people

beliefs   symbols
(Christianity)
ceremonies   key people

CO-OPERATIVE SKILLS

The roles of editor, illustrator, proofreader were demonstrated, as well as methods of providing feedback to peers. Jane played a role game (see page 61) to show the importance of roles we play in groups. Feedback stressed the notion of criticising the ideas presented and not the person or personality of the writer.

SESSION 10: INDIVIDUAL RESPONSIBILITY

Until this session there had been no problems with individual responsibility within groups until Bill had trouble finding the resources he needed. Bill was in a group researching Christianity. Specifically, his group wanted to research the role of the priest. He complained that he couldn't find the information the group required in any book in the library. The group called a meeting to help Bill solve the problem of not doing the work. The group:

• asked Bill to explain why he hadn't done the work
• made decisions about what were legitimate reasons
• helped Bill modify his questions so he could find resources
• helped Bill call in a priest because he couldn't find the information he needed in books.

The groups had allocated specific questions to individual students which meant that no one in the group could freeload on another's work. The group needed Bill's information and worked positively with him to help solve the problem of lack of information.

SESSIONS 11–13: FINAL DRAFTS

The final drafts of the research projects came in from pairs and individuals. Editors and proofreaders within each group took responsibility for typing up the finished fact booklet on one religion in the Middle East. Jane photocopied the final product.

FINAL SESSION

JIGSAW

Jane used a jigsaw structure, developed by Aronson et al. (1977) to organise this final session. Jigsaw begins with students in expert research groups gathering information. Once the research groups have enough information to answer the research questions, they are reorganised into co-operative groups. Each co-operative group member in Jane's class was an expert on each religion — Islam, Judaism and Christianity.

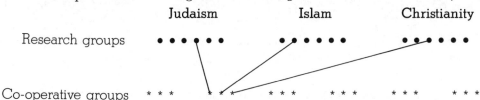

The co-operative groups shared the research information they had gathered. Each co-operative group of three compiled and summarised information on the religions in the Middle East and created a board game or a leaflet.

ASSESSMENT

The school has a policy that grades of A–E be given for all curriculum areas. Individuals were assessed for the information, use of research skills plus co-operative skills, receiving a total of 70 marks.

Jane talked with each student and individually negotiated the 50 marks for each section of the research process.

- forming research questions
- finding information
- note taking
- organising information
- presentation of information

There were 20 marks set aside by Jane for co-operative skills based on how individuals worked together. A group may get 15 marks and each group would add the 15 to their individual score. Individuals also assessed their own use of co-operative skills and received 5 additional points if they thought their behavior warranted this. The groups assessed themselves on questions such as:

- How did I work with others?
- What did I contribute?
- What are my strengths?
- What do I need to work on?
- Did I dominate?
- Did I encourage others?

IN SUMMARY

Jane states that once the research projects got underway,

> . . . the amount the class needed me was minimal. They were clear about the research project which was in small simple steps. The teacher plays the role of troubleshooter and encourager. I don't accept the responsibility of solving the problems as by setting up the co-operative structures they can solve the problems themselves.

The jigsaw structure used in this co-operative research project is a way of organising so that all students are accountable for their own learning. When students go to the co-operative groups, they are the only person in the group with the specific information gathered in their research team. Students cannot freeload on each other's efforts as each person has a small jigsaw piece of information to provide for their group.

Throughout each session Jane reminded the class about using co-operative skills. Feedback at the end of each session showed the class that Jane valued co-operative skills enough to set aside precious time for this.

FEEDBACK

In Jane's class positive feedback to each person is important. Knowing we belong to a group and are accepted helps build cohesion.

WHIP

This feedback idea is a quick response to how people worked in a group by 'whipping around the group'. Encouraging everyone to make a statement also fosters individual accountability.

AFFIRMATIONS

Each person in the group writes their name on a large sheet of paper and passes the paper to the person next to them. That person writes a positive statement about how that person worked.

> *Bill shared his research idea ideas.*
> *Sarah helped me work out a problem.*
> *Robbie showed me how to get to the library.*

After the positive comment is written, the paper is folded and passed to the next person until the sheet is filled with positive affirmations and is returned to the original owner. These affirmation sheets can be referred to when things get tough.

SUGARGRAM

We all find it hard to give and receive positive feedback and honest compliments. Participants sit in a circle and write a positive and honest compliment to as many people as possible. Remind children not to write a compliment to just the most popular people as everyone should have at least one compliment. When the compliment has been written fold it, walk over make eye contact and give it to the person. Compliments can be about behaviour:

> *Sam took turns.*
> *You listened carefully.*
> *You helped me solve a problem.*

Some of the compliments may appear superficial but use this to discuss how the more we give positive feedback the easier and more honest. There is no doubt that giving and receiving such feedback is pleasurable.

Participants should not open their sugargrams until everyone has one.

FUNNY FEEDBACK

This is a humorous way to get feedback as people raise their fingers in response to questions. It is practically impossible to raise your ring finger when all other fingers are clenched.

Ask each person to place the knuckles of their right hand down on a flat surface. Tell the group that you are going to ask four questions and if the answer is *Yes*, they are to raise their thumb or finger.

1. Were you actively involved as a group member? If yes, raise your thumb.
2. OK. Thumb down. If you encouraged others to work in some way raise your little finger.
3. Finger away. Now for the forefinger or index finger. If you listened to others raise this finger.
4. Finger away. Now listen carefully and raise your ring finger if the answer is yes. Are you really good at co-operative learning?

People will laugh as they try to free the ring finger to hold it up. This is a good icebreaker or freeing up activity. You can only use it once. (Scannell & Newstrom 1983)

100

SUMMARY

Academic ability and achievement alone do not ensure success in life. A gifted reader, physicist or mathematician requires knowledge of how to work and communicate with others and the skills to work co-operatively.

We do not do it alone. The scientist works in a team. Teachers, counsellors, lawyers and parents realise that to get the work done and to move forward we need the co-operative skills necessary to work together. We have enough social and intellectual challenges over the next decades to make us strong. Working together and building on each other's positive strengths is essential if we are to tackle successfully the technological, scientific and social changes that lie ahead.

School does not have to be a tough competitive place. We do not need tough, competitive, emotional and social experiences to make us strong. The old rhyme, *Sticks and stones may break my bones but names will never hurt me*, is simply not true. Names do hurt. It's the names we remember.

Helping children to play, work and manage conflict together requires us to shift our focus to the co-operative nature of how we work. Competition has traditionally been seen as the motivation for a few to perform at the expense of others. It is now time to view co-operation for all as a dynamic, productive way to grow and learn.

REFERENCES

Aronson, E., Blaney, N., Stephan, C., Sikes, J. & Snapp, M. 1977, *The Jigsaw Classroom*, Sage Publications, Beverly Hills, Cal., USA.

Aronson, E. 1980 in *Cooperation in Education*, eds S. Sharon, P. Hare, C. D. Webb & R. Hertz-Lazarowitz, Brigham Young University Press, Utah.

Cohen, E. 1990, 'Continuing to co-operate: Prerequisites for persistence', *Phi Delta Kappan*, October, pp. 134–8.

de Bono, E. 1991, *Handbook for the Positive Revolution*, Viking, London.

Delbecq A.L & Vande Ven, A.H. 1971, 'A group process model for problem identification and program planning', *Journal of Applied Behavioral Science*, vol.7, no. 4, pp. 466–91.

Dishon, D. & Wilson, P. 1991, 'It looks easier than it is', *Co-operative Learning Magazine*, vol. 11, no. 3, pp. 45–6.

Fluegelman, A. 1978, *The New Games Book*, Sidgwick and Jackson, London.

Fountain, S. 1990, *Learning Together*, Stanley Thornes.

Graves, N. & Graves, T. 1990, *A Part to Play: Tips, Techniques and Tools for Learning*, Latitude Media, Melbourne.

Hill, S. & Hill, T. 1990, *The Collaborative Classroom*, Eleanor Curtain Publishing, Melbourne.

Hill, T. & Reed, K. 1989, 'Promoting social competence in preschool: The implementation of a co-operative games program', *Australian Journal of Early Childhood*, vol. 14, no. 4, pp. 25–31.

Johnson, R. & Johnson, D. 1985, *Co-operative Learning: Warm Ups, Grouping Strategies and Group Activities*, Interaction Book Company, Edina, Minnesota.

Johnson, R. & Johnson, D. 1989, *Cooperation and Competition: Theory and Research*, Interaction Book Company, Edina, Minnesota.

Johnson, R. & Johnson, D. 1990, 'What is co-operative learning?', in *Perspectives on Small Group Learning: Theory and Practice*, ed. Brubacher et al., Rubicon Publishing, Canada.

Kagan, S. 1990, *Cooperative Learning: Resources for Teachers, Resources for Teachers*, San Juan Capistrano, Cal., USA.

Katz, L. & Chard, S. 1989, *Engaging Children's Minds: The Project Approach*, Ablex Publishing Corporation, Norwood, NJ, USA.

Kriedler, W. 1984, *Creative Conflict Resolution*, Scott Foresman and Company, Illinois, USA.

Lankshear, C. 1991, 'Getting it right is hard: Redressing the politics of literacy in the 1990s', *Australian Reading Association Selected Papers*, ARA, South Australia.

Laurence, D. 1987, *Enhancing Self-Esteem in the Classroom*, Paul Chapman Press, London.

Maguire, J. 1990, *Hopscotch, Hangman, Hot Potato and Ha, Ha, Ha: A Rule Book of Children's Games,* Prentice Hall Inc, New York.

Masheder, M. 1990, *Let's Play Together*, McCulloch Publishing, Melbourne.

Orlick, T. & Botterill, C. 1975, *Every Kid Can Win*, Nelson Hall, Chicago, USA.

Orlick, T. 1981, *The Second Co-operative Sports and Games Book*, Pantheon Books, New York.

Pax Christi 1980, *Winners All*, St Francis of Assisi Centre, London.

Phillips, J.D. 1948, 'Report on Discussion 66', *Adult Education Journal*, vol. 7, pp. 181–2.

Piaget, J. 1977, *Development of Thought: Equilibration of Cognitive Structures*, trans. A. Rosin, Viking.

Rinvolucri, M. 1986, *Grammar Games: Cognitive, Affective and Drama Games for EFL students*, University Press, New York.

Scannell, E.E. & Newstrom, J.W. 1983, *More Games Trainers Play*, McGraw Hill Book Co., New York.

Slavin, R. 1985 'An introduction to co-operative learning research', in *Learning to Co-operate: Co-operating to Learn*, eds R. Slavin, S. Kagan, R. Hertz-Lazarowitz, C. Webb & R. Schmuck, Plenum Press, New York.

Slavin, R. 1989, *Co-operative Learning: Theory, Research and Practice*, Prentice Hall Inc, New York.

Wells, G., Chang, M. & Maher, A. 1990, 'Collaborative inquiry and literacy', in *Perspectives on Small Group Learning: Theory and Practice*, ed. M. Brubacher et al., Rubicon Publishing, Canada.

INDEX OF GAMES AND ACTIVITIES

Books for Co-operative Learning

The Collaborative Classroom: A Guide to Co-operative Learning
Susan and Tim Hill   ISBN 1 875327 00 2   illustrated 162pp

A creative and practical guide which focuses on and identifies the areas where co-operative skills are needed: forming groups — working as a group, problem solving as a group; and managing differences — discussing problems, offering suggestions and providing practical applications.

There are dozens of activities to get the beginning teacher started.

Becoming Responsible Learners: Strategies for Positive Classroom Management
Joan Dalton and Mark Collis   ISBN 1 875327 05 3   illustrated 80 pp

An extremely practical and highly readable book on strategies and guidelines for classroom management, resulting from the authors' observations of effective collaborative teachers at work, and conversations with them about their beliefs and classroom practices.

The book is an invaluable asset to teachers who want to encourage children to take responsibility for their own learning and behaviour.

Raps and Rhymes
Selected by Susan Hill   ISBN 1 875327 03 7   illustrated 80pp

This is a stimulating selection of traditional chants and rhymes that have been played with, improvised on and read by children of all ages. Reading aloud as a group or joining in a chant or a rhyme is a great warm-up to any lesson, and an effective way to build up a feeling of cohesiveness in class.

There are selections for improvising, clapping and clicking, action rhymes, part-reading, and just plain nonsense rhymes.

Readers Theatre: Performing the Text
Susan Hill   ISBN 1 875327 01 0   illustrated 88pp

Readers theatre is a simple, informal and motivating way to involve students in the study of literature by group storytelling, shared reading, improvisation and performance of a favourite story.

This book provides complete scripts for performance, guidelines for helping children write their own scripts, aids and ideas for improvisation, and lists texts that work well in adaptation.

For information on these and other titles contact
Eleanor Curtain Publishing
906 Malvern Road, Armadale 3143, Australia
Tel (03) 822 0344 Fax (03) 824 8851

Distributed in New Zealand by
Ashton Scholastic
165 Marua Road, Panmure, Auckland
Tel (09) 579 6089 Fax (09) 579 3860